UNIVERSITY OF **ILLINOIS** PRESS

REVIEW COPY

Passing for Spain
Cervantes and the Fictions of Identity
Barbara Fuchs

U.S. Cloth Price: $32.50
Publication Date: February 10, 2003

Contact: Danielle Wilberg (217) 244-4689

Please send TWO copies of your review to:

University of Illinois Press
1325 South Oak Street
Champaign, IL 61820-6903
Fax: (217) 244-8082   AUG 2 7 2003

Passing for Spain

Hispanisms

Series Editor

Anne J. Cruz

*A list of books in the series appears
at the back of this book.*

Passing for Spain

Cervantes and the Fictions of Identity

Barbara Fuchs

University of Illinois Press
Urbana and Chicago

Publication of this book was supported by a grant from the Program for
Cultural Cooperation between Spain's Ministry of Education and Culture
and United States Universities.

♾ This book is printed on acid-free paper.

Library of Congress Cataloging-in-Publication Data
Fuchs, Barbara.
Passing for Spain : Cervantes and the fictions of identity /
Barbara Fuchs.
p.   cm. — (Hispanisms)
Includes bibliographical references and index.
ISBN 0-252-02781-7 (cloth : alk. paper)
1. Cervantes Saavedra, Miguel de, 1547–1616—Criticism and interpretation.
2. Passing (Identity) in literature. 3. Gender identity in literature. 4. Identity
(Psychology) in literature. 5. Disguise in literature.
I. Title. II. Series.
PQ6358.I43F83   2003
863'.3—dc21   2002004978

Para Nico, que jamás pasará desapercibido,
y para las Señoras Montenegro

Costume and custom are complex.
The headgear of the other sex
inspires us to experiment.

—Elizabeth Bishop, "Exchanging Hats"

Contents

Preface:
Serious Play

Mi intento ha sido poner en la plaza de nuestra república
una mesa de trucos. [My intention has been to place
a billiards table in the square of our republic.]
—Miguel de Cervantes Saavedra, *Novelas ejemplares,* "Prólogo al lector"

Sabes lo que comúnmente se dice, que debajo de
mi manto, al rey mato. [You know the popular saying,
that under my cloak, I kill the king.]
—Miguel de Cervantes Saavedra, *Don Quijote,* part I, "Prólogo"

Despite their tongue-in-cheek, bantering tone, Cervantes's prologues provide tantalizing hints of a *mode d'emploi* for his texts. The billiards table, with its seemingly random permutations and combinations, is located squarely in the middle of the commonwealth, as though to encourage the reader to think through the larger implications of textual bumps and jolts and other authorial tricks. The offhand reference to discreet regicide, for its part, invites a knowing reader who will be an accomplice to the text's ironic mode and its political nuances.

These two opaque but suggestive moments preface my own reassessment of Cervantes's playfulness with genre and of the slipperiness of disguise in his texts. While critics have long recognized Cervantes's generic legerdemain, they have read it largely in formal terms. The problems of disguise and identity—also widely recognized—have received ample critical attention as examples of perspectivism or the carnivalesque but have rarely been considered within the ideological matrix of Counter-Reformation Spain. To use Cervantes's terms, critics have focused on the billiards table and the cloak but not on the square or the king. This book proposes a historically situated vision of these two modes of textual play, introducing the concept of *passing* as a challenge to the strictures of Counter-Reformation orthodoxy.

My argument considers two modes of passing simultaneously. First is a literary passing that disguises an acute concern with pressing historical and social issues under the veil of conventional, idealized modes. Such formal passing functions as a kind of generic irony, calling attention to the historical and political disarray that lies beneath the cloak of literary conventionality. Second, I address a form of transvestism that extends well beyond gender to cross ethnic, religious, and national boundaries. This cultural cross-dressing, which I trace historically to the vexed Mediterranean frontier between Christianity and Islam, complicates the construction of a national identity for a newly unified Spain, replacing the notion of fixed, genealogically determined subjects with much looser, performative selves. In *Passing for Spain* I argue that the seemingly playful and often highly pleasurable scenes of cross-dressing and disguised identity in Cervantes's texts mount a grave challenge to the verities of Counter-Reformation ideology. The play of disguise thus becomes deadly serious as it takes on such crucial issues as the conceptual and ideological limits of the emerging nation and the conflictive construction of viable identities within Spain.

⌒

This project began under the watchful eye of Alban Forcione and Timothy Hampton. Stephen Orgel first urged me to publish a version of chapter 2, which appeared in *Cervantes* 16 (Fall 1996). Patricia Parker and Diana de Armas Wilson enthusiastically supported the project from that early stage with their insight and generosity. Several audiences of *cervantistas* and early modern scholars at the University of Washington and elsewhere helped me refine the argument. Carroll Johnson, whose own work has been most inspiring, kindly read an early chapter. David Quint gave me both encouragement and constructive criticism. George Shipley read the entire manuscript and provided invaluable suggestions at every point. Marshall Brown generously offered his insight and support. Various chapters also benefited from readings by my Pacific Northwest writing group: Stephanie Camp, Jeffrey Collins, Joy Connolly, Jeannine DeLombard, Catherine Sanok, and Dan White. My research assistants—Heather Easterling, Daniel Phillips, and Brooke Stafford—provided valuable help, while the University of Washington Royalty Research Fund afforded me the time to complete the manuscript. Jennifer Macdonald kindly provided me with a copy of the video project *Passing* that she and Hillary Leone created.

The editors of *PMLA* offered many useful suggestions for chapter 3, which appeared in slightly different form in volume 116, number 2 (March 2001) of that journal. At the University of Illinois Press, Anne J. Cruz and Willis G. Regier have been unfailingly helpful. I would especially like to thank Professor Cruz and the Press's anonymous readers for their insight. Finally, my deepest thanks go to Todd Lynch, my staunchest and best reader.

Passing for Spain

Passing and the Fictions of Spanish Identity

Imagining Spain

Given the various pressures of centralization, imperial ambition, and religious dissidence, the construction of national identity in early modern Spain was an enterprise fraught with difficulties. As a reaction to the peninsula's long-term occupation by Islam, and to bolster its claims to the New World, sixteenth-century Spain ostentatiously assumed the mantle of Defender of the Faith—main bastion of a beleaguered Catholicism and Christian nation par excellence. The conflation of the fall of Granada to the Catholic kings, the expulsion of the Jews, and Columbus's arrival in Hispaniola in 1492 served as a triple landmark on the road to consolidation and expansion. As Philip II's monarchy aligned itself with Counter-Reformation orthodoxy, the elaboration of a national myth based on a "pure" Christianity took on greater urgency. While the monarch promoted himself as champion of the true Church against heretics and infidels, a new vein of humanist historiography conveniently occluded Spain's Moorish past and touted an unchanging "Gothic" nation that stretched back to pre-Roman times.[1]

It is important to underscore that this sense of early modern Spain as a homogeneous nation reunited through the Reconquista was a myth, challenged not only by the prominence of hybrid subjects, especially *conversos,* in many areas of public life but also by the many tensions between local allegiances and centralizing forces.[2] The emphasis on a pure Christian genealogy was an early aspect of Spanish nation-formation—in Etienne Balibar's useful terms, an attempt to construct the "fictive ethnicity" that would hold together an "ideal nation."[3] As Balibar argues,

> The history of nations, beginning with our own, is always already presented to us in the form of a narrative which attributes to these entities the continuity of a subject. . . . The illusion is twofold. It consists in believing that the generations which succeed one another over centuries on a reasonably stable territory, under a reasonably univocal designation, have handed down to each other an invariant substance. And it consists in believing that the process of development from which we select aspects retrospectively, so as to see ourselves as the culmination of that process, was the only one possible, that is, it represented a destiny.[4]

Balibar emphasizes the deliberate selection and construction of an identity from the materials available in the historical *longue durée.* In the case of Spain, this process involved erasing all traces of Moorish and Jewish cultures to focus on an illusory ancestral Gothic nation as the substratum of early modern Spain.

The Spain I refer to here is a nation in the making—by no means a fully achieved nation-state, but instead a polity in the throes of centralization and modernization, struggling to base a strong state on an older sense of an ethnic or genealogical *natio.* The tension between the older and newer meanings of this nation—a term that Covarrubias succinctly (and tautologically) defines as "reyno o provincia estendida, como la nación española" (an extended kingdom or province, such as the Spanish nation)[5]—is precisely what concerns me here. Who belongs within the Spanish nation? And how are its limits to be determined?

Over the course of the sixteenth century, state and church gradually defined some of those limits by excluding descendants of Moors and Jews from positions of power within civil and religious institutions through the infamous *estatutos de limpieza de sangre* (blood purity statutes). While there is some disagreement among historians about the true breadth or import of the statutes, it is clear that the problems of *limpieza* loomed large in the culture's imagination.[6] As critics from Américo Castro on have pointed out, a broad range of Spanish texts evince a pervasive anxiety about *limpieza* and its attendant distinctions. The possibility of making these distinctions depended on subjects being transparent and classifiable—as though past religious or ethnic affiliations really did equal a manifest physical difference. In fact, *limpieza* could not be so easily determined, because in pillorying or clearing individual subjects there were often larger interests at stake—economic considerations, tensions between regional structures and the monarchy's centralizing drive—as well as personal animosities. Furthermore, the subjects in question were often quite deliberately unreadable, and the categories in which they supposedly belonged were themselves problematized by their ambiguity. Despite the rampant stereotypes that attempted to pigeonhole Spain's Others and all the Golden Age jokes about big noses, pork products, and wine, religious identity in Counter-Reformation Spain was never really crystal clear. In the case of the

Moriscos—the Moors who remained in Spain after the fall of Granada and were converted, often forcibly, to Christianity—the anxiety about the authenticity of their conversions and the impossibility of determining whether they were merely simulating their allegiance to Spain compounded the economic and political struggles over their allegiance. Over the course of the sixteenth century, the state passed a series of increasingly repressive laws against Moorish cultural practices aimed at erasing all traces of the Moriscos' ethnic identity.[7] These measures culminated with the expulsion of the Moriscos from Spain (1609–14), a final attempt to rid Spain of a class of subjects whose perceived intractable difference—despite their actual assimilation—precluded their inclusion in the homogenized "ideal nation" imagined by Counter-Reformation orthodoxy.

In this book I address the representation of unreadable subjects in the pervasive scenes of "passing," or deliberate impersonation, in Cervantes's texts. I argue that his depictions of characters who effectively perform another gender or religion challenge the attempt to identify and categorize "proper" Spanish subjects. As these characters move between ostensibly disparate and impermeable categories—masculine and feminine, Moor and Christian, Turk and European—they call the categories themselves into question. Even as Spain becomes increasingly intolerant of ethnic and religious differences within its population, these literary scenes of passing suggest the impossibility of drawing rigid boundaries between often indistinguishable subjects. Cervantes's fictions thus present a challenge to the enterprise of national consolidation according to essentialized hierarchies. By reading backward from scenes of passing to the larger social text of Counter-Reformation Spain, I examine, first, the resistant fluidity of individual identity in the period and, second, the ways in which that fluidity undermines a collective identity based on exclusion and difference.

Normative, aristocratic male subjects in Counter-Reformation Spain staked their identity on two basic tenets: *honra* (honor) and *limpieza de sangre* (blood purity). The first depended largely on male valor and female chastity, as well as on stringent distinctions between classes. The second was based on equally trenchant distinctions between Old Christians—ostensibly untainted by Semitic blood—and New Christians—*conversos* and Moriscos who had recently converted to Christianity. Moreover, the two notions were interconnected: through the sustained equation of the East with effeminacy and of Semitic peoples with women, masculinity was erected into a crucial aspect of Spanish identity.[8] As Josiah Blackmore and Gregory Hutcheson argue, *limpieza de sangre* and *honra* "are ultimately manifestations of the same master discourse, the conflation of notions of purity and orthodoxy into a reflexive impulse against the threat of racial, cultural, and sexual queerness (and the desires invoked by each)."[9]

While these tenets were important for individual identity, they were equally crucial for the sense of a national self. Over the course of the sixteenth century, Spain attempted to construct a collective identity based on an ancestral devotion to Christianity—guaranteed by the erasure of the Jewish and Moorish taints—and a muscular defense of the faith. Just as individual identity was hardly experienced in an uncomplicated fashion, however, the incipient national identity was riddled with contradictions. What was an ostensibly homogeneous Spain to make of regional differences, highly influential converts, or its humbling military defeats as the champion of the true Church? The fractured nature of the emerging national identity suggests how literary depictions of confused boundaries and protean subjects might counter both the exclusionist version of Spain and the state's attempts at ethnic classification.

Cervantes's representations of passing present precisely such a challenge to the state's categorization of persons. I focus on Cervantes not only because of the central place his texts have occupied within the canon of Spanish letters but because they consistently engage the problems of the nascent Spanish nation. The historical context for Cervantes's literary career accounts in part for his complex treatment of passing. His production spans the period from the rebellion of the Moriscos in 1569 to their final expulsion from the peninsula in the first two decades of the seventeenth century. It thus coincides with the period of greatest anxiety over blood purity and the heightened operations of the Inquisition after the Council of Trent, as well as with the increasing displacement of Morisco populations within Spain and the larger Mediterranean area. This is also the period when the enormous domestic costs of maintaining Spain's empire become apparent and of widespread disillusion with Spain's imperial enterprise.

This vexed and conflicted polity is abundantly reflected in Cervantes's texts. Many apparently conventional scenes of cross-dressing are situated at the border of a highly unstable Spain, portrayed as a nation vulnerable to bandits, pirates, and other forms of lawlessness. In these scenes transvestism—in its etymological sense of "dressing *across*"—often signals not only gender indeterminacy but a far more territorial crossover between self and other, underscoring the porosity of national boundaries and the fragility of an identity predicated on masculinity and blood purity. Thus the traditional purview of transvestism or cross-dressing expands to reach across established categories of gender, religion, and nationality. I argue that Cervantes foregrounds passing as a way to question the fixity of cultural identity precisely in ambiguous episodes of rescued captives, renegades, escapes from the Moors, and so forth. Their identities veiled, even constructed, by disguise, the characters who pass complicate what it means to belong within Spain.

The power of cross-dressing (in this broader sense) to challenge an exclusionist version of Spain makes perfect sense when one considers the historical importance of dress to mark—or blur—identities. In her analysis of "fashioned subjectivity," Claire Sponsler reminds us that "clothing is a complex sign, one that is open to multiple and conflicting interpretations, interpretations often arrived at under the oversight of powerful and vested interests. Although clothing might seem to promise instant recognition of others, their social condition, and their relation to the viewer's self, it often leads to confusion, deception, and misrecognition as well."[10] Sumptuary laws, such as those passed repeatedly in early modern Spain, attempted to control the disorder of dress by stipulating, for example, that only those who kept horses could wear silk.[11] The ordinances were repeated over the course of the sixteenth century, voicing an acute concern over the expenses incurred for lavish dress. The last decree passed by Charles V complained of the many garments of brocade and cloth of gold "'allí en nuestra corte como fuera de ella'" (both within our court and outside of it), an excess "'que es causa de que muchos gasten sus haçiendas y hay mucha desorden y nuestros reinos se destruyen y empobrecen'" (that leads many to waste their property, and there is great disorder and our kingdoms are destroyed and impoverished).[12] Ultimately, the sumptuary laws were insufficient to contain the mobility that clothing could afford.

In his dictionary, Covarrubias offers a definition of *vestidura o vestido* (clothing or dress) that evinces his anxiety over the categorizing of a national costume in a time of changing fashions and the muddling of class lines through sartorial excess:

> Todas las naciones han usado vestiduras propias, distinguiéndose por ellas unas de otras; y muchas han conservado su hábito por gran tiempo. A los españoles en este caso nos han notado de livianos, porque mudamos traje y vestido fácilmente. Y assí el otro que se hazía loco, o lo era, andava hecho pedaços y traya al ombro un pedaço de paño, y preguntándole porqué no se hazía de vestir, respondía que esperava a ver en qué paravan los trajes. Solo los labradores, que no salen de sus aldeas, han durado más en conservar el traje antiguo, aunque ya esto también está estragado. . . . No es instituto mío tratar de reformaciones, pero notorio es el exceso de España en el vestir, porque un día de fiesta el oficial y su muger no se diferencian de la gente noble.[13]

> [All nations have had their own dress, which distinguishes them from others, and many have preserved their costume for a long time. In this regard, Spaniards have been noted as fickle, because we change habit and dress with such ease. And so a fellow who was mad or pretended to be, running around in rags with a cut of material over his shoulder, when asked why he did not have clothes made from it, would answer that he was waiting to see where fashion would end up. Only

the peasants, who do not leave their towns, have kept the old costume for longer, but even this is now spoiled. . . . It is not my business to deal with reform, but the excess of dress in Spain is notorious: on a holiday, an official and his wife are indistinguishable from nobles.]

Whereas Covarrubias seems particularly concerned with the erasure, through dress, of national and class distinctions, Lope de Vega's *El caballero de Olmedo* (1620; The knight of Olmedo) longingly recalls fifteenth-century attempts to separate Jews and Moors from Christians by marking their clothing. The orthodox yearning for clear markers of difference where religion is concerned is projected backward, to the reign of Juan II (1406–54), who appears in the play mainly to proclaim the separation of Jews and Moors from Christians. This separation will be guaranteed, or so the play would have it, by clothing:

> a manera de gabán
> traiga un tabardo el judío
> con una señal en él, y un verde capuz el moro.
> Tenga el cristiano el decoro
> que es justo: apártese dél;
> que con esto tendrán miedo
> los que su nobleza infaman[14]

[For a cloak, let the Jew wear a tabard with a badge on it, and let the Moor wear a green cape. Let the Christian behave with the appropriate decorum by maintaining his distance from them, for this will strike fear into those who would slander his nobility.]

Strikingly, even as the king legislates the difference of Jews and Moors, he acknowledges the vulnerability of "proper" Christians to accusations of tainted blood.

Despite Lope's nostalgic evocation of sartorial difference, in the fifteenth and early sixteenth centuries it was quite fashionable for Christian Spaniards to dress as Moors.[15] Was this a perverse nostalgia for remnants of Islamic Spain? In some cases, as when a group of young dancers dressed *a la morisca* welcomed the future emperor Charles V on his first trip to Spain,[16] Moorish attire paradoxically functioned as a sign of national identity—an identity predicated on the erasure of Spain's Moorish past. In a related fashion, Moorish dress was regularly adopted for ceremonial occasions such as the *juegos de cañas*—a jousting game of Moorish origin—or mock battles that celebrated victories over Moorish enemies. In these cases, ethnic cross-dressing and the performance of ersatz Moorishness contribute to the construction of a "fictive ethnicity" for Spain as a nation that has overcome Islam in part by fetishizing its visible manifestations in the context of ceremonial performances. As such, these performances enable the construction of identity by staging otherness.[17] Yet Moorish or Moorish-derived dress was not only ceremonial; it was also often part of everyday attire, from headdresses (through the reign of Charles V) to women's undergarments. Ultimately, then, such attire marks the porosity between Moorish and Spanish identities and Christian Spain's sustained fascination with its own Moorish past—both phenomena that continued long after the fall of Granada. Evidently, the orthodox mania for ethnoreligious purity and the classification of subjects coexisted with an enduring enchantment with Islam and cultural crossovers.[18] One of the clearest signs of this fascination is the genre of the *novela morisca,* from *El Abencerraje* (1561, 1562, 1565) to *Ozmín y Daraja* (1599). As critics repeatedly point out, despite their Moorish garb the protagonists of these fictions are often indistinguishable from the courtly knights and ladies of chivalric romance. While they might be read as Christians passing for Moors rather than as meaningful representations of Islamic subjects, they also introduce the chiasmic possibility that actual Moors could pass for Christians.

In a culture obsessed with identifying difference through outward signs, dress became a loaded marker of identity for all involved: if Christian Spaniards could playfully dress up as Moors, then the persecuted and ostracized Moriscos could also pass as "real" Spaniards. Given this historical context, Cervantes's depiction of characters who cross cultural boundaries through disguise—such as the Morisca Ana Félix, in *Don Quijote,* who dresses up as a corsair captain but proclaims her Christianity throughout[19]—complicates the notion of essential differences between Spaniards and their others. The passing in these texts exposes the contradictions of Spanish policy over the course of the sixteenth century, from violent efforts to make the Moriscos abandon their cultural practices—rendering them, to all appearances, indistinguishable from Christians—to their ultimate banishment from Spain. Most important, passing challenges the very notion of a transparent, easily classified identity on which the state can rely for exclusionary purposes.

Cervantes's depiction of passing in a Counter-Reformation context evinces the complexities of identity and nation-formation in the period. In recent years, scholars have begun exploring the construction of racial difference in medieval and early modern Europe and the connections among gender, theatricality, and community.[20] Francesca Royster, for example, suggests that the depiction of racial passing in Shakespeare's *Titus Andronicus* reflects a deep cultural anxiety about impostors and invasion, a concern with "a kind of encryption, a hiding of true natures, whether racial, barbaric, or moral; such encryption enables Goths and Moors to infiltrate Rome and plays on fears of an infiltrated England."[21]

In a New World context, recent studies on colonial "Spanish" society identify from the earliest period of the Conquista until the late eighteenth century the phenomenon of "racial drift"—the change in the racial label attached
to subjects between their baptismal and their marriage records—so that wom-
en who were born mestizas, for example, might become "Spaniards" upon
marrying a Spanish male, effectively passing from one category to another.[22]
Elizabeth Anne Kuznesof convincingly shows how gender and race were fundamentally interconnected in the New World, with women far more likely to
undergo a conceptual whitening as a result of their marriage unions. As Kuznesof points out, "The 'race' and 'gender' of individuals varied in value and
meaning based on historical choices and opportunities and the way in which
these things interacted and were interpreted in colonial documents and by
colonial populations."[23] Perhaps the most flamboyant case of deliberate gender choice in colonial Latin America is the transvestite ensign-nun Catalina
de Erauso, whose myth has been exhaustively analyzed by Sherry Velasco.[24]

Such transformations were not the exclusive preserve of the colonial world,
however. Israel Burshatin examines the figure of Eleno de Céspedes, an Andalusian slave who essentially rewrote her/his own story through "corporeal
and sartorial transformations wrought on a stigmatized body, transforming
herself from domestic slave to soldier and surgeon, from subservient female
to proud transgendered subject." Burshatin describes how, in the charged
context of Andalucía, Eleno's transgressiveness as an empowered, brown-
skinned male led to his arrest as a suspected *monfí*, or Morisco outlaw. The
threat of such bandits, Burshatin suggests, lay precisely in their ability to pass
as Old Christians and to move easily between Muslim and Christian worlds.[25]

Despite these promising contributions, there is much work to be done on
the precise imbrications of gender, religion, and incipient notions of race with
emerging national identities. While Josiah Blackmore and Gregory S.
Hutcheson's collection *Queer Iberia* is an important exception, the studies that
have been most explicit about these connections generally focus on contemporary or modern cultural productions. In a U.S. context, critics such as Eric
Lott and Michael Rogin consider the importance of passing for nation-formation, yet their focus is on minstrelsy—a kind of passing in which the artifice
is transparent. Here, the marginalized race is enacted by mainstream perform-
ers or by third parties who want to assimilate into the mainstream.[26] In Rogin's terms, this kind of "passing down" involves subjects who, as perform-
ers, have a choice in the roles they play: "the more the freedom to perform any
role, the less subversion in the play."[27] Rogin's argument counters the more
liberatory reading of passing in Marjorie Garber's work, in which the figure

of the transvestite marks a "category crisis . . . a failure of definitional distinction, a borderline that becomes permeable, that permits of border crossings from one (apparently distinct) category to another: black/white, Jew/Christian, noble/bourgeois, master/servant, master/slave."[28]

Garber's broad survey often sacrifices contextual nuance, but her theoretical insight is crucial: through analogy, one kind of crossing may stand in for another, enabling the veiled representation of truly subversive possibilities and challenging the very categories used to classify subjects. While Garber does not make the distinction between passing *down* and passing *up*, her discussion of minstrelsy is framed by a larger discussion of racial passing and transvestism by blacks in search of freedom or economic opportunity, implicitly suggesting that any full account of passing must necessarily include marginalized subjects as well as hegemonic ones who playfully adopt marginal identities. In recent criticism, passing up is most often associated with the Harlem Renaissance's highly individual, often tragic accounts of subjects whose impersonations exact a high psychic cost, as in the novels of Nella Larsen. Yet in these cases the category of the national often falls out of the analysis.[29] In *Passing for Spain* I demonstrate how very pertinent performative notions of identity are to a much earlier period, and to its particular version of nation-formation, by stressing the category crisis that gender and ethnoreligious passing pose for a masculinist, Christian Spain.

It is not my intention to portray Cervantes as a philosemite. Instead, I argue that his texts constantly de-emphasize and problematize essence, suggesting an openness toward the convincing *performance* of Spanish identity instead of an obsession with transparency and genealogy. While this emphasis contrasts markedly with the prevailing Counter-Reformation orthodoxy and reveals the transgressive possibilities paradoxically enabled by fixed categories, one must cautiously avoid a celebratory reading, especially given the painful reality of the Morisco expulsions. The danger of passing, as of the implicit acceptance of others who are willing to perform the hegemonic identity, is that actual cultural difference may disappear. In real terms, passing may involve eventual assimilation and the loss of identity. Yet once the long-term fragility of passing subjects—and the impasse that passing ultimately represents for the marginalized culture—are recognized, the inconclusiveness of stories like that of Ana Félix acquires a different valence. Those stories become most powerful and resonant in presenting the unresolved question of belonging and identity: passing effectively casts repressive categories into crisis, even if it does not necessarily resolve intolerance or afford permanent accommodation within the boundaries of a narrowly imagined Spain.

Negotiating the Mediterranean

Early modern Spain's most vulnerable and unstable boundary was the line dividing it from Islam. After the fall of Granada in 1492 and the end of the Nasrid kingdom, the line is conventionally drawn at Spain's Mediterranean coastline, but the reality of the frontier was far more complex.[30] Spain faced the continued presence within its borders of the Moriscos, forcibly converted to Christianity but always suspected of an underlying allegiance to Islam. Yet the protracted hostilities between Christianity and Islam on this frontier co-existed with frequent commercial exchanges. Thus entire classes of subjects crossed this porous frontier, both on the peninsula and throughout Spain's Mediterranean empire. Exiles, deserters, corsairs, captives, renegades (either willing converts or those forced to convert in captivity)—these often overlapping groups gave the lie to any clear distinction between Europe and Africa or between Christianity and Islam.[31] Within the overdetermined Mediterranean contact zone, their layered identities—whether performed or "authentic"—seriously complicate any account of religious or national allegiance in the period.

As I argue above, early modern Spain attempted to distinguish itself from Islam in no uncertain terms through the emphasis on a genealogically verifiable Gothic identity for true Spanish subjects, the increased persecution of the Moriscos, and the construction of a national myth that cast Spain as heir of imperial Rome and defender of the Church. Yet the actual vagaries of Mediterranean identity in the period involved a great deal more intermingling and hybridity than the official story acknowledged. Cervantes's representation of this complexity in scenes of religious and ethnic passing emphasizes an open Mediterranean, in striking contrast with the ostensibly closed Spain of Counter-Reformation ideology. His emphasis on the permeability of the contact zone and on the fluidity of the subjects who inhabit it effectively undoes the orthodox narratives of homogeneous and fully realized national identity put forth by the Spanish Crown.

Miguel de Cervantes Saavedra experienced the dangerous proximity of Christianity and Islam in his own person after being captured by corsairs on his way back to Spain following the battle of Lepanto. His early depictions of Algiers, in his play *Los tratos de Argel,* were probably written while he was still a captive in order to raise money for redemptions.[32] The North Africa of *Los tratos* is a world of stark differences between stalwart Christians, such as the significantly named Saavedra, and apostates who endanger their souls if they even pretend to betray their faith. In between lies only the class of forced renegades—captive children melodramatically torn from their parents' arms in scenes designed to tug at the heartstrings.[33] While this vision emphasizes the threat of Islam to an often fragile Christian identity, it also corresponds neatly to the demonization of Islam in Counter-Reformation ideology.

Yet, as Cervantes returns again and again to the portrayal of Islam, in both *comedias* and *novelas,* as well as in the parts I and II of *Don Quijote,* the representations become increasingly complex. Instead of the pronounced differences between Europe and Africa, they emphasize the sustained possibilities for religious dissimulation on the part of subjects located between the two and the resulting confusion of national boundaries and categories. Moreover, they underscore Spain's prolonged aesthetic fascination with all things "Oriental," which promotes the above confusion through the mechanisms of fetishistic consumption. In the two cases that I discuss in chapter 4, the novella "El amante liberal" (translated as "The Generous Lover") and the later play *La gran sultana Doña Catalina de Oviedo,* the unorthodoxy of these representations is somewhat softened by locating them far from Spain, in the eastern Mediterranean, where Turks replace Moors as Christians' primary antagonists. These locales are the scene of various dubious transactions of commerce and identity as both renegades and counterrenegades proliferate. In part II of *Don Quijote,* however, Cervantes returns us to Spain to consider the problems of heterogeneity and belonging within the metropolis itself. As I suggest in chapter 2, in Sancho's former neighbor Ricote—a wine-drinking, Spanish-speaking Morisco expelled by royal order yet surreptitiously back in Spain disguised as a pilgrim—and his ironically named daughter, Ana Félix, who passes as a Moorish corsair, Cervantes gives us hugely sympathetic characters whose uncertain status within Spain simply cannot be resolved. The open-ended, ambiguous fate of Ricote and his daughter suggests the limitations of official policy. Thus Cervantes's depictions of the Mediterranean in-between underscore its complexity when they reflect historical reality but also when they pointedly differ from it, as in the representation of a more accepting Spain in which punishment or re-expulsion would not be the immediate consequence of the Moriscos' discovery by Spanish authorities.[34]

What does the historical record tell us about passing between Christianity and Islam in the period? Recent studies have emphasized the frequency of European contacts with Turks and Moors, whether through diplomatic and commercial missions or more informal channels.[35] In the case of Spain, the expulsion of the Jews in 1492 and the gradual Moorish diaspora from the fall of Granada to the mass expulsions in the early years of the seventeenth century produced a steady stream of subjects who crossed the line, willingly or otherwise. A fascinating anonymous *relación* from 1617 gives some sense of the complexity of these passages. When four Christian galleys capture a flotilla of

Turkish vessels, they liberate Christian captives and take Turkish and Moorish prisoners, among whom is one chameleonlike couple. I quote at length to give the full sense of the complexity of the transformations involved:

> Entre las mugeres que se cautivaron auia vna moça de buen talle, que puesta delante del General, en lengua Española dixo: que aunque estaua en habito Turquesco, eran de Lisboa ella, y su marido que estaua en la cadena, al que traxeron luego alli, y preguntandole, como siendo Español andaua en aquel habito? Respondio, que aunque el, y su muger, que estaua presente, hauian nacido en Lisboa, eran hijos de Hebreos, y que prendiendo a sus viejos padre, y suegro, vn tio de su muger los despachó para Seuilla con mas de siete mil ducados en letra, y que passados quatro meses tuuieron auiso de Lisboa, que se fuessen a Italia, porque sus padres negociauan muy mal: y dando el dinero a vn Genoues, les dio letra para Genoua, y que cortandose el cabello su muger, y en habito de hombre se embarcaron en Alicante para Genoua, y tomando alli letra de su dinero para Venecia, viuieron alli dos años, y que por tener vn primo hermano de su padre en Constantinopla, se auian venido el, y su muger a viuir con el. La portuguesa que era de muy buen rostro, y muchacha, que en todo este tiempo auia estado llorando, le dixo al marido, que pues auia empeçado a dezir verdades, que no mezclase mentiras: y boluiendose al General dixo: Señor, yo he sido muy engañada, que aunque soy hija de Hebreo, siempre he viuido como Cristiana, mi padre por fuerça me casó con este hombre, que yo con Cristiano viejo queria casar: ya casada con el, tomele amor, y amor me hizo dexar a España, y en ageno habito acompañarle hasta Venecia, alli me dixo el traydor que viniesemos a Constantinopla, adonde en llegando renegó, y compró vn Genizarato, y el Cacis [Cadí?] me hizo renegar a mi por fuerça: pero en el coraçon tengo a Dios, y a su Madre: yo tengo mi merecido por casarme con un perro Iudio. Luego el General mando que le boluiessen a la cadena, y que a ella se le tratasse muy bien.[36]

[Among the women whom they captured was a young and comely one who, brought before the general, said to him in Spanish that although she was wearing Turkish garb she was from Lisbon, as was her husband, who was chained to the oars. They brought him forth immediately and asked him how it was that he wore such attire if he was a Spaniard. He answered that although he and his wife, who was present, had been born in Lisbon, they were the children of Jews and that when their old father and father-in-law had been arrested, his wife's uncle had sent them to Seville with a money order for more than seven thousand ducats, and that after four months they had word from Lisbon that they should go to Italy because their fathers' affairs were going very poorly. And giving their money to a Genoese, he gave them a money order for Genoa; and that his wife cut off her hair and, dressed as men, they set sail from Alicante to Genoa; and there procuring a money order for Venice, they lived in that city for two years, and that because a cousin of his father's lived in Constantinople, both he and his wife had come to live with him. The Portuguese woman, who was very beautiful and young and who had been crying this entire time, said to the husband that since he had begun by telling truths he should not mix in lies, and turning to the general she said: "Sir, I have been much deceived, for although I am the daughter of a Jew, I have always lived as a Christian. My father forced me to marry this man, for I wanted to marry an Old Christian. Once married to him, I grew to love him, and my love made me leave Spain and accompany him to Venice in another's attire. There the traitor said we should go to Constantinople, where he reneged as soon as we arrived and bought a post as a Janissary. The Cacis forced me to renege, but in my heart I hold God and his Mother; I have gotten my just desserts for marrying a Jewish dog." Then the general ordered he should be chained again to the oars and that she should be treated very well.]

The protagonists of this amazing encounter, with its strange echoes of the Ana Félix story, are virtually protean. While their gold changes from one money order to another, marking the financial interconnectedness of European states, they themselves cross different kinds of lines, changing vertiginously from Spaniards to Portuguese to Jews to Turks. Amid the bewildering transformations, the woman's cross-dressing seems almost incidental, as the notion of *ageno hábito* in terms of gender is ironized by their constant changes of costume as they pass and renege. A combination of religious persecution, family ties, and financial expediency renders them double or triple agents who pass as necessary to ensure their survival. The transformations come to an end with the wife's intimate betrayal of her husband, whom she accuses of being a traitor. Yet the tantalizing possibility remains that her convenient confession may be no truer than the story he offers, despite the rhetorical privileging of her voice as a direct quotation. After all, his narrative does not provide much of a rationale for mercy from their Spanish captors, while her tale of forced conversion and enduring devotion to Christianity immediately affords her better treatment at their hands. In the end, the story seems to turn on gender as much as religion, as the wife, whose beauty is repeatedly noted, emphasizes her passivity at every turn, even when forced to dress as a man.

While the *relación* relies on the reader's sympathy for the wife as a forced renegade, many Christians, like her Jewish husband, crossed over willingly to Islam. The *turcos de profesión* (Turks by profession), as Diego de Haedo calls them, came from every corner of Europe, from Russia to Scotland to Castile.[37] Renegades provided the Muslims with technological and military expertise, particularly in artillery.[38] In Christopher Marlowe's *Tamburlaine I* (1590), Bajazeth the Turk crows that he has as many "'warlike bands of Christians renied, / As hath the ocean or the Terrene Sea / Small drops of water'" (3.1.9–11). And the *Letters from the Great Turke Lately Sent unto the Holy Father the Pope* (1606) boast of renegades fighting "'in defence of our lawe, and with us to conquer your country.'"[39] While some of these renegades had probably been captured in eastern Europe as young children and formally trained as Janissaries, others were western Europeans who chose to join Muslim troops for the favorable treatment they received. Spain's North African outposts proved especially vulnerable to the lure of Islam. After consolidating its power on the peninsula in 1492, Spain attempted to reinforce its position against the Moors by establishing a series of garrisons on the Barbary Coast. Isolated and remote, the presidios proved very difficult to supply or defend, becoming "one of the great mirages of Spanish frontier policy."[40] As the situation in the presidios became ever grimmer, large numbers of soldiers chose to desert from these forsaken outposts, voluntarily going over to Islam.[41]

Other Christians who crossed over had more specific motives. Some of the cases recorded by the Inquisitional tribunals, with their odd mix of romance and Mediterranean realpolitik, are reminiscent of Cervantes's later fictions. To take just two of the most striking examples: in 1610, the Andalusian Francisco Martínez followed a Grenadine Morisca to whom he was betrothed to North Africa; and in order to join his captive beloved, the Sicilian Pietro Polimeno willingly boarded a Turkish ship that was negotiating ransoms (despite his sacrifice, she eventually left him for another man).[42] The echoes of Ana Félix and her Old Christian lover Don Gregorio and of the spurned Ricardo ("El amante liberal") in these accounts are quite striking. Although it is unlikely that they served as sources, they locate Cervantes's fictional narratives squarely within the historical context of the Mediterranean and of the vexed negotiation of identity in such a contested space.

The most spectacularly successful class of renegades were the corsairs, who led countless *razzias* against European ships and coastal towns throughout the Mediterranean and eventually in the Atlantic. The corsair societies of North Africa largely depended upon European renegades, who found ample opportunities for enrichment and economic advancement once they converted. The most famous of the corsairs, from the Barbarossa brothers on, were renegades. Thus, while piracy made travel between Christianity and Islam far more dangerous and expensive, the corsairs themselves crossed the line with great success. The Moriscos, with their truly hybrid culture, proved particularly adept at moving back and forth across the shifting frontier. Forcibly baptized and acculturated, yet subsequently expelled from Spain for their Moorish blood, Morisco corsairs could pass as Spaniards, using their detailed knowledge of Spanish coasts and of the Spanish language to trick their victims. This passing confirms that there was often no "manifest truth of melanin," in Amy Robinson's felicitous phrase,[43] to mark the Moriscos—or, indeed, North African Moors or Turks—as racial others in the modern sense, despite the occasional European theatrical indexing of these groups with blackface.[44]

The success of the corsair raids accounts for the huge number of captives who moved, albeit forcibly, between Christianity and Islam. While some, especially young children, were forced to apostatize, others chose to do so of their own free will, attracted by the economic or social advantages of conversion. Still others were ransomed by redemptionist religious orders who canvassed constantly for the huge sums of money required.[45] Here again the case of the Moriscos appears to be particularly interesting: so indistinguishable were they from "real" Spaniards that they complicated the negotiations for redeeming captives from North Africa. In a move that unwittingly challenged the rationale for the expulsions themselves, the state instructed the redemptionist religious orders to "watch with great vigilance that the captives you redeem are not Moriscos expelled from this kingdom."[46] Like the Morisco corsairs, these captives were only passing as what they in fact had been until the expulsion decrees stripped them of their Spanish identity by fiat.

Because Christian corsairs also participated in this alternative form of warfare, captives were taken on both sides.[47] Some of the most interesting cases of passing, amply documented in Inquisitional archives, involve renegades who, after being captured by Christians and taken aboard their ships, attempted to hide the fact that they had ever been Christians themselves.[48] Unless they were denounced by their own shipmates, or by previously redeemed captives who had known them in North Africa, they stood a good chance of dissimulating their origins. The stakes were high: as Turks or Moors they would be sent to row in the galleys but could hope to be ransomed; as renegades, they would be brought before the tribunals of the Inquisition and face the full weight of its sanctions. Far from being a fixed category, therefore, these subjects' ethno-religious identification seems to have been strategically determined according to specific circumstances. As renegades and captives on both sides of the Christian-Muslim frontier navigate the complex waters of Mediterranean identity, they suggest how radically that identity may shift in response to particular locations or repressive contexts.

These large classes of passing subjects show that performative notions of identity are by no means the prerogative of our own time—that is, they apply also to the period of intense social and political reorganization around the consolidation of early modern states and the intensification of religious persecution in the Counter-Reformation. Passing strategically rehearses supposedly stable markers such as language, class, "race," ethnicity, religion, and nationality, thus complicating any possibility of categorical classification. And the performed identities clearly exist beyond the confines of the stage or of literature more generally: passing subjects proliferate outside any text or set of generic conventions. The practice appears even more widespread than either contemporary literary representations or the Inquisitional records—which, after all, mark instances of *failed* passing—would suggest.[49] The cases I discuss here should therefore be understood not as marginal phenomena within Cervantes's texts but rather as textual indexes of a much larger concern with the policing of borders and of identity in the early modern Mediterranean world.

Because this contingent and strategic performance of identity is crucially involved with survival, it is always passing up. That is, this kind of passing does not involve a hegemonic group enacting otherness for the purposes of consolidating a national, racial, or religious self, as in the *juego de cañas,* or mock battles, discussed above. Instead, those marginalized by the consolidation of that self disguise themselves either to achieve inclusion—as in the case of the Moriscos attempting to be redeemed from North Africa and repatriated to Spain—or to escape religious persecution—as with the renegade Christians passing as born Turks. My argument thus concerns a very different class of actors than those considered by Clark and Sponsler, who ask: "Was it possible that through discourses and representations articulated around visible signs of otherness (clothing, skin color, religious rituals) and 'put on' in the course of dramatic performances, the social body could take a racial other into itself and through such incorporation enact both transgression and preservation from all forms of invasion, disruption, and dissolution?"[50] As the authors' own analysis of medieval drama clearly shows, the answer is a resounding yes. Yet it is also the case that unwitting incorporation could occur through the agency of the other and unbeknownst to the social body, in which case the emphasis clearly falls on transgression rather than preservation. Thus, while all literary representations of passing help reconstruct the complexity of identity in the period, it behooves us to consider those instances that seem to undo or challenge stereotypes as well as the more familiar instances that reinscribe them.

Staging Genres, Staging Genders

If, as I argue above, Cervantes constructs representations of gender and ethnoreligious passing that challenge the hegemonic sense of Spain, why do those representations not provoke greater controversy? The answer, I think, is twofold. First, the identity of even normative male, aristocratic Spanish subjects is so fragile that it leads to a kind of conspiracy of silence, only occasionally breached by those who dare point out that the emperor has no clothes. This is exactly the situation that Cervantes parodies in the Old Christian, rich peasant setting of "El retablo de las maravillas," where the respectable townspeople would rather be duped by *pícaros* than admit they cannot see the "miracle" on stage, which purportedly guarantees their Old Christian identity. As I suggest in my reading of the *Persiles* in chapter 5, even the rich and powerful within Spain were vulnerable to accusations of unclean blood, which could entirely destroy them.[51] Beyond the widespread anxiety about blood purity, moreover, the lower echelons of the aristocracy were often involved in complex economic charades. Like the hapless squire in *Lazarillo de Tormes*—or, arguably, Alonso Quijano himself—they frequently led a life of acute economic deprivation in order to maintain a social status that offered concrete financial advantages, such as avoiding taxation, but that threatened to collapse at any moment under the weight of financial reality. Thus Cervantes's representation of passing at the margins often taps into much more widespread anxieties about the social order within Spain itself and about the sustainability of any identity held to orthodox norms.

The second reason has to do with the specific formal strategies of Cervantes's representations. Their transgressive quality is elusive: they are often qualified by orthodox endings, pointed irresolution, or moments of ventriloquism in which marginalized characters voice the ideology that condemns them. At such moments, Cervantes relies on a devastating irony to get his message across while shielding his text from official persecution. More important, he deploys literary convention—the iteration of recognizable tropes, albeit in significantly divergent contexts—to disguise the power of his own critique behind a veil of conventionality. Cervantes's texts about passing are often passing themselves, as their form reproduces the protective strategies of disguise and dissimulation described in their content.

The most frequent strategy in this formal passing is the use of conventional romance topoi. Modern critical neglect of Cervantes's so-called idealist texts—the *Persiles*, the "Italianate" novellas—stems from the misprision of his formal strategies of passing, which serve to defuse the radical questions that the texts pose.[52] While the *Persiles* and novellas such as "El amante liberal" were very popular throughout the seventeenth and eighteenth centuries, twentieth-century critics—especially those working within a comparative or non-Hispanic framework—overwhelmingly privileged the "realist" Cervantes, chronicler of alienation and so-called father of the modern novel. This construction of Cervantes makes the romance texts an aberration or a perplexing regression. Alternatively, critics argue that the romance texts must actually have been written before *Don Quijote* instead of at the end of Cervantes's life.[53] Even a critic invested in dislodging this implicit hierarchy argues that Cervantes's romances involve a "lessened importance of social criticism" and suggests that beyond their fiction lies "a social order serenely confident of itself."[54]

Although scholars such as E. Michael Gerli, Diana de Armas Wilson, Carroll B. Johnson, and George Mariscal have greatly contributed to our historical understanding of Cervantes's idealist texts, little work has been done to reexamine their representation of gender and ethnoreligious transgression in light of the nationalist enterprise of Counter-Reformation Spain. The critical recognition that Cervantes often plays with the contrast between the ideal and the real, and among competing literary genres, is here reconsidered in historical terms to argue that romance form dissimulates a very pointed and precise critique of Spain.[55] My intent is thus to assess the specific historical implications of Cervantes's literary strategies. In the less familiar texts I discuss here ("Las dos doncellas" [The two damsels], "El amante liberal," *La gran sultana,* the *Persiles,* and "La española inglesa" [The English-Spanish girl]), hyperconventional romance tropes—idealized protagonists, unlikely coincidences, pirates and bandits—cloak a minute engagement with pressing historical and social questions of gender, nation, and empire.

Both *Don Quijote,* which most fully ironizes literary conventions, and the so-called idealist texts play constantly with genre and gender as Cervantes manipulates not only narrative traditions but the conventions of stage transvestism. The encounter in the *Persiles* between the disguised heroine, Sigismunda/Auristela, and a wandering playwright ironically illustrates the appeal of cross-dressing on stage and off, as he imaginatively disrobes her and dresses her in a variety of seductive male costumes:

> Digo, en fin, que este poeta . . . fue el que más se admiró de la belleza de Auristela, y al momento la marcó en su imaginación y la tuvo por más que buena para ser comedianta, sin reparar si sabía o no la lengua castellana. Contentóle el talle, diole gusto el brío, y en un instante la vistió en su imaginación en hábito corto de varón; desnudóla luego y vistióla de ninfa, y casi al mismo punto la envistió de la majestad de reina, sin dejar traje de risa o de gravedad, de que no la vistiese, y en todas se le representó grave, alegre, discreta, aguda, y sobremanera honesta: estremos que se acomodan mal en una farsanta hermosa.

> [In short, I say again that this poet . . . was the one most astonished by Auristela's beauty. She immediately stuck in his mind, and, not giving a thought to whether or not she knew the Spanish language, he felt she'd be more than good as an actress. He was pleased by her figure, he liked the way she carried herself, and in his mind's eye he dressed her in a flash in a man's short suit, next he stripped her and dressed her as a nymph, then almost in the same instant clothed her with the majesty of a queen. There wasn't any comic or tragic costume in which he didn't dress her, and in all of them he imagined how she'd look acting

serious, carefree, wise, witty, and exceedingly modest, opposites not usually found in a beautiful entertainer.][56]

As contemporary critics of the theater would certainly have pointed out, transvestism signifies the erotic. The inspired poet gains access to Auristela's body by imagining her in male costume, progressing from the transvestite fantasy to successive imaginative disrobings and recostumings. Yet, ultimately, the cross-dressing actress represents a *discordia* that never quite becomes *concors;* she cannot represent many roles and at the same time maintain an appearance of female decorum.

As an acute observer of contemporary culture, Cervantes is well aware of the intense fascination that cross-dressing holds for an audience. Lope de Vega, in his "Arte nuevo de hacer comedias en este tiempo" (1609) (New art of playwriting in our time), rather ambiguously advises women to avoid giving offense by cross-dressing while acknowledging the appeal of such performances:

Las damas no desdigan de su nombre;
y si mudaren traje, sea de modo
que pueda perdonarse, porque suele
el disfraz varonil agradar mucho.[57]

[Ladies should not go against their name; and should they change clothes, let them do it in such a way as may be forgiven, because the male costume is often very pleasing.]

Lope's directions acknowledge the scandalous excess of transvestism on the Spanish stage. Unlike in England, where boys made up for the lack of female players, women in female roles were generally tolerated in Spain. But instead of solving the problem of transvestism, their presence led to a proliferation of cross-dressing plots.[58] As Ursula Heise points out, in Lope's and Cervantes's Spain, "plays whose romance plots require women to dress in men's clothing become so overwhelmingly popular that antitheatrical writers and stage legislation see themselves forced again and again to address the question of the legitimacy of female cross-dressing before a public audience."[59] Some of the most fascinating examples of this cross-dressing, such as Tirso de Molina's *El vergonzoso en palacio* (1612–13) or *Don Gil de las Calzas Verdes* (1615), radically challenge the prevailing gender ideology by suggesting that masculinity is a sartorial fiction.[60] In general, however, the most transgressive moments in theatrical cross-dressing are somewhat qualified by the anagnorisis at the end, which reveals the female identity of the transvestite. While this kind of resolution does not entirely undo the gender trouble of the cross-dressing scenes, it generally encloses it within a frame of restored order. Moreover, the relative conventionality of actresses cross-dressing, as evinced by the poet's fantasy in the *Persiles* and by Lope's knowing admonition in his "Arte nuevo," further limits any real challenge that they might pose.

In Cervantes's *comedias*, however, conventional stage transvestism often gives way to more complex crossings of gender, religious, and ethnic lines.[61] As I discuss in chapter 4, *La gran sultana* features a subplot in which a *male* captive dresses as a woman in order to follow his beloved into the sultan's seraglio. When caught, "she" claims that Islam has endowed "her" with miraculous masculinity: upon converting, "her" timeless wish to become a man was granted by Mohammed. At such moments, Cervantes sutures the conventional and the scandalous, gender identity and religious affiliation, depicting a greater permeability not only between genders but, crucially, between Christianity and Islam. The imbrication of the religious divide with constructions of masculinity and effeminacy—Christianity is masculine and warlike; Islam, soft and weak—is thereby both upended and ironized. In these scenes, transvestism no longer signifies mere dressing as the other gender; instead, it effects a more profound move across established categories of gender and religion, veiling ideological certainties with various layers of sartorial (mis)identification.

Cervantes also exploits the phenomenal popularity of stage transvestism in order to script transgressive scenes of passing in his prose. As I show in chapters 2 and 3, the scenes of cross-dressing in *Don Quijote* and "Las dos doncellas" combine the conventional romance motif, wildly popular on the stage, with far more complex representations of epic androgyny. As part of this generic bait and switch, Cervantes locates the scenes of passing at Spain's borders, invoking epic's focus on nation and empire building while complicating gender, religious, and national categories. These texts, I suggest, must be read in the broader context of Spain's large and conflictive empire, not only in the New World and the Pacific, but also in Flanders and Italy, with its almost unsustainable expanse and extended border with Islam. In this context, the play of genre and of gender in Cervantes's fictions intersect to pose larger questions about Spanish masculinity and about who belongs within Spain's empire and how their essential allegiance may be proved. In these texts, the border itself is problematized by a deliberate disorder that transcends it: both Spain and its margins are inhabited by characters who pass in order to perform often contradictory identities, undoing any efforts at easy categorization. As the following chapters show, the complexity of individual passing subjects and their multilayered performance of identity expose the fiction of a collective national identity predicated on singularity, transparency, and homogeneity.

2

Border Crossings:
Transvestism and Passing in *Don Quijote*

The disjunction between truth and fiction in *Don Quijote* has often been cir-cumscribed as a literary problem: how is Don Quijote interpreting the world around him as a literary text; and, conversely, how does that world resemble literature? Yet there are moments of deception in *Don Quijote* that require deciphering within the social text of Counter-Reformation Spain—a text in which the distinctions between appearances and reality are often much more nuanced than in the romances of chivalry that constitute Cervantes's prima-ry literary referent. Reading the perspectivism of Don Quijote's literary mad-ness is relatively simple: when he takes sheep for armies, or windmills for gi-ants, he explains the disjunction between what *seems* and what *is* as the work of enchanters. As Michel Foucault points out, Don Quijote's quest includes a built-in justification for his failure to find a reality that reflects the romances of chivalry: "So all the indices of non-resemblance, all the signs that prove that the written texts are not telling the truth, resemble the action of sorcery, which introduces difference into the indubitable existence of similitude by means of deceit. And since this magic has been foreseen and described in the books, the illusory difference that it introduces can never be anything but an enchanted similitude, and, therefore, yet another sign that the signs in the books really do resemble the truth."[1]

Yet what of those transformations in the text that function as antisorcery, introducing similitude where there should be difference? Located outside Don Quijote's main sphere of operations and distinct from his chivalric madness, these transformations have more to do with Cervantes's depiction of gender norms and religious categories. They cast doubt on our initial perceptions as readers—things are not what they seem to be—as they disturb the self-identity of gender and nation in the novel. By confusing the lines of difference and pointing out its constructedness, such transformations introduce a principle of ambiguity into the rigid binarisms of Spanish orthodoxy: male versus female, Christian versus Moor, masculine versus effeminate. The alchemy I allude to is transvestism. The several instances of cross-dressing, mainly in part II of *Don Quijote,* work their peculiar magic on the novel's gender economy and on the construction of Spanish selves in opposition to Moorish others.

The most striking cases of transvestism in *Don Quijote* occur in marginal spaces of lawlessness—the Sierra Morena, the frontier—or in Sancho's Insula Barataria—a fictional realm of difference in which political authority is constantly interrogated. Instead of merely upending the stability of gender, these episodes reflect the anxieties surrounding the sexual, political, and religious limits of Spain. The various kinds of difference confounded by transvestism become especially charged when those differences challenge the nation at its borders; by conflating them, Cervantes airs such anxieties without explicitly positing effeminacy or religious plurality within Spain. The conflation depends on the commonplace attribution of sodomy to Turks and Moors, as part of their othering, and on the romance and epic traditions of cross-dressing and border crossing that Cervantes draws on for his text.

In his depiction of female-to-male transvestism, Cervantes conflates two earlier traditions: the wandering cross-dressers of romance and the "martial maids" of epic.[2] The former, with its conventions of escape from danger or love intrigue, largely responds to the exigencies of plot: at the end comes a resolution that re-establishes the normative order of things, usually through the discovery of the disguise. This romance transvestism, with its spectacular possibilities for anagnorisis, proved irresistible for the Spanish as well as the English theater.[3] As Heise points out, transvestism was no less common on the Spanish stage than on the English, even though the appearance of women in female roles was generally tolerated in Spain. Unstable gender identities on the stage provide a controlled titillation, ultimately resolved within the theatrical frame, yet even such limited and reversible transformations produce an incredible anxiety among critics of the theater.[4]

Cervantes's use of such plots exploits the fantastic popularity of these devices while exploring the potential of narrated (versus staged) transvestism. For although the "reality" of the staged, immediate cross-dressing might seem transgressive in its actuality, it is disarmed by the theatrical frame. The end of the play brings the end of the ambiguity. Narrated transvestism, by contrast, introduces a principle of uncertainty: though not as vivid, it disseminates cross-dressing beyond the stage, so that in fact any beautiful young man may be a woman in disguise and every personable young lady a beardless gallant. Moreover, although the main theatrical traditions involve female-to-male transvestism, Cervantes examines also male-to-female cross-dressing, thereby interrogating the construction of gender in broader terms. By destabilizing a basic category of apprehension and social organization, he complicates readers' perceptions of reality: while Don Quijote goes on about windmills and enchanters, a more pervasive genre of transformations is afoot.[5]

Much Ado about Beards

The earliest instance of cross-dressing in the novel both invokes and inverts the parameters of romance transvestism. Determined to bring Don Quijote home from his mad ramblings in the Sierra Morena, the curate and the barber decide to embody a chivalric fantasy in their own persons. The curate announces he will dress up "en hábito de doncella andante" (276) (in the costume of a wandering damsel), while the barber, to the best of his ability, must dress up as her squire, "y que así irían adonde Don Quijote estaba, fingiendo ser ella una doncella afligida y menesterosa, y le pediría un don, el cual él no podría dejar de otorgar, como valeroso caballero andante" (276) (and that they would go thus to where Don Quijote was, with her pretending to be an afflicted and needy damsel, and would ask of him a favor, which he, as a valiant knight, could not but grant). The plan recalls the common romance conceit of the cross-dressed damsel in distress, except with a peculiar twist: here, it is the curate who must disguise himself in order to impersonate a damsel in proper female attire.

Maese Nicolás, for his part, takes on a *masculine* disguise that underscores the constructedness of gender and the artificiality of its outward forms. This disguise seems particularly striking in a text that features several *marimachos,* or masculine women, who possess an excess of masculinity. What seems a given in a character such as Aldonza Lorenzo, the "moza . . . de pelo en pecho" (262) (lass . . . with hair on her chest), whom Don Quijote insists on transforming into his Dulcinea, is scrupulously constructed in this episode.[6] While the curate is carefully dressed by the hostess in *saya* (petticoat) and *corpiños* (blouse), the barber's costume consists largely of a huge borrowed red beard, crafted from the tail of an ox, "donde el ventero tenía colgado el peine" (277) (where the innkeeper hung his comb). Beards, of course, have traditionally been associated with virility and honor and are a basic mark of gender difference.[7] The nature of the disguise suggests that the significance of the barber as a main character goes beyond the humor of the *baciyelmo* episode (I.21), in which Don Quijote takes another barber's bowl for the magical helmet of the Moor Mambrino, from Boiardo's *Orlando innamorato* (Orlando in love). In fact, the constant reference to beards and barbers provides Cervantes with an opportunity to examine the construction of masculinity itself. *Hacerse la barba* (to have one's beard done/made)—the innocent procedure mentioned in the *baciyelmo* episode (207)—gradually comes to suggest the artificiality of male identity. In the Sierra Morena, the fetish-beard serves to mark an abundant masculinity that distinguishes the barber from the effeminized curate. Yet the vicissitudes of this borrowed beard, which refuses to stay on, signal a masculinity that is as easily dropped or lost as it is sported. With its insistence on this prop of masculinity, the entire episode suggests, in Judith Butler's cogent formulation, that the "abiding gendered self" is structured "by repeated acts that seek to approximate the ideal of a substantial ground of identity, but which, in their occasional discontinuity, reveal the temporal and contingent groundlessness of this 'ground.'"[8]

As soon as the disguises are complete, the curate has second thoughts: deciding that it is *cosa indecente* (an indecency) for a priest to dress thus, he convinces Maese Nicolás to exchange costumes, but then he proceeds to instruct the patient barber in proper feminine behavior—a lesson the latter claims not to need (278). The interchangeability of gender in this episode suggests just how malleable the category is: the two friends not only feel certain they can play a female role, but their familiarity with chivalric literature provides them with what they consider an appropriate script for femininity. Yet Cervantes qualifies the disruptive potential of the male-to-female cross-dressing by replacing it with the more proper romance mode well known to his audience. The curate and the barber, in their disguises, encounter the cross-dressed Dorotea, an actual woman who will save both of them from transvestite impersonation. Although Dorotea's own adventure is fairly conventional, it narrowly averts a most unusual plan.

Dorotea wears her male costume from necessity (and not very well at that), in order to find Don Fernando, the nobleman who seduced and then abandoned her. The normal order of things has been altered by betrayal and dishonor; her transparent transvestism is just one more sign of that disorder. Dorotea's disguised flight into the Sierra Morena can be compared to the escapes in male guise of Shakespeare's comic heroines, such as Rosalind or Viola, who respond to a disordered world by changing gender roles and taking on a manly appearance for their own protection. But, unlike these, Dorotea does not preserve her independence or her "masculine" resolution for long. Her discovery by the barber, the curate, and Cardenio leads instantly to the revelation of her femininity. Dorotea's game is up almost immediately, and she resumes both her female identity and the deference and helplessness that are supposed to accompany it. The three men first hear a lament in which the speaker refers to herself as *desdichada* (293) (unhappy woman). After this early signpost of female identity, Cervantes launches into the conventions of voyeurism and titillation often associated with cross-dressing: the men espy a young peasant washing "his" dazzlingly white feet in a stream and letting down "his" beautiful hair (294).[9] Although the curate courteously keeps up some pretense of doubt about Dorotea's gender, he addresses her within the conventions of chivalry:

—Lo que vuestro traje, señora, nos niega, vuestros cabellos nos descubren: señales claras que no deben de ser de poco momento las causas que han disfrazado vuestra belleza en hábito tan indigno, y traídola a tanta soledad como es ésta, en la cual ha sido ventura el hallaros, si no para dar remedio a vuestros males, a lo menos para darles consejo, pues ningún mal puede fatigar tanto, ni llegar tan al extremo de serlo, mientras no acaba la vida, que rehúya de no escuchar, siquiera, el consejo que con buena intención se da al que lo padece. Así que, señora mía, o señor mío, o lo que vos quisierdes ser, perded el sobresalto que nuestra vista os ha causado y contadnos vuestra buena o mala suerte: que en nosotros juntos, o en cada uno, hallaréis quien os ayude a sentir vuestras desgracias. (295)

["What your costume would conceal, Madam, your hair reveals to us: sure signs that it can be no slight cause that has hidden your beauty in such an unworthy disguise and brought you to this desolate spot, where we have been fortunate enough to have found you, if not to dispel your miseries, at least to offer advice, for no affliction save death can be so great that one should refuse to listen to the counsel given in all goodwill to those who suffer from it. So, my lady or my lord, whichever you prefer, do not be startled by the sight of us and tell us of your good or evil fortune so that we may express our sympathy for you, either all together or singly."]

Despite his gesture of deference to her gender ambiguity, the curate clearly underscores Dorotea's femininity. Under her male attire, the damsel in distress is abundantly revealed, as Dorotea acknowledges that her costume is ineffective and, moreover, that it requires a narrative to justify her actions and neutralize the danger she is in:

—Pero, con todo esto, para que no ande vacilando mi honra en vuestras intenciones, habiéndome ya conocido por mujer y viéndome moza, sola y en este traje, cosas, todas juntas, y cada una por sí, que pueden echar por tierra cualquier honesto crédito, os habré de decir lo que quisiera callar, si pudiera. (360)

["Yet as I do not wish you to speculate about my honor, now that you have recognized me as a woman and see me, young, alone, and in these clothes—circumstances that together or individually are enough to destroy any honest reputation—I shall tell you what I wish I could keep quiet."]

Cross-dressing tarnishes Dorotea's *honra,* and the discovery of her disguise relocates her as a passive female who must appeal to men and participate in the patriarchal conventions of honor and female chastity if she is to seek redress. The cross-dressing is limited to a crisis situation, and the disadvantages of Dorotea's male disguise are clear: it is easily pierced by male observers, casts a shadow on her virtue, and exposes her to the unwanted attentions of those, such as her own servant, who assume that she has donned promiscuity along with her male hose.

When Dorotea chooses a less transgressive costume, casting herself as the fabulous Princess Micomicona to help get Don Quijote home, the situation becomes clearly ironic: not only is Dorotea in her "real" identity a woman in distress (although no longer technically a *doncella,* or virgin), but her self-definition signals her complete relinquishment of a "masculine" role in her own cause, along with her masculine costume. Yet the containment does not entirely erase the transgressive effects of cross-dressing, for Dorotea's fortuitous appearance to play Micomicona recalls the original plan—by which first the curate and then the barber would cross-dress as the damsel in distress— even as it improves upon it. And the chivalrous rescue, in this case, seems to go both ways: the men will play the role of saviors if Dorotea will save them from effeminization.

Moreover, with the Micomicona plot a peculiar form of racial passing replaces Dorotea's gender transformation. The curate initially introduces her as coming from Guinea (310), but Sancho quickly changes her provenance, making her "queen of the great kingdom of Micomicón in Ethiopia" (315). Her ostensible origins and Sancho's unsavory speculations about her black subjects, whom he will transform into *blancos o amarillos* (314) (white or yellow, i.e., silver or gold) by selling them into slavery, recast Dorotea as the curiously pale ruler of an African realm. She recalls Tasso's Ethiopian princess, Clorinda, in *Gerusalemme Liberata* (Jerusalem delivered)—an African who was born white because her pregnant mother gazed on a painting of a chivalric St. George saving a white virgin from a dragon.[10] As David Quint convincingly shows, Tasso's ambivalent portrayal of Clorinda reflects both the European excitement at discovering an actual Christian kingdom in Africa—and thus a potential ally against Islam—and the subsequent disillusion with the divergent practices of Coptic ritual, which made Ethiopian Christianity at least as heretical as Protestantism.[11]

In Cervantes's version, the religious dimension is largely elided, although the sense of an Ethiopia more in need of European succor than able to aid Christianity against Islam comes across in Micomicona's plea for help against the giant who has usurped her kingdom. Sancho's mercenary ruminations do, however, complicate the correspondences between religion and race. His readiness to imagine enslaving presumably Christian black subjects from Ethiopia recalls the controversial Spanish exploitation of marginalized Christians, whether the persecuted Moriscos in Spain or the natives of the New World. Even more striking is the fluidity of racial identity in Dorotea's "disguise" as a white African princess—a fluidity that reprises the gender constructedness so emphasized in the cross-dressing plots. A number of details strengthen the connection between racial/religious passing and transvestism at this early stage of the novel: the *baciyelmo* that originally served to "make beards" and that Don Quijote so longs to wear is, in his fantasy, a Moor's helmet; and the enormous red beard that constitutes Maese Nicolás's disguise is reprised in the tale of the Captive, who refers repeatedly to the famous renegade corsair Barbarroja (420)—a far more troubling example of passing for Africa than either Dorotea's role or the mad knight's Moorish headdress.

Even when the need for female disguise has been obviated by a "real"— though pale—Micomicona, Cervantes returns again and again to this beard as a fetishized sign of masculinity. The larger-than-life appendage first falls off, astounding Don Quijote, who eagerly requests the recipe for the balm that can heal a face and reattach a beard so easily (316). Then the curate, as himself, explains his lone travels by recounting an attack by the same galley slaves that Don Quijote had injudiciously freed, who "nos quitaron hasta las barbas; y de modo nos las quitaron, que le convino al barbero ponérselas postizas" (318) (stripped us to our beards; and even took them, so that the barber had to put on a false one). His tongue-in-cheek reference to the mobile disguise literalizes the proverbial *hasta las barbas* and once again suggests a masculinity that comes off easily, only to be as easily replaced by an artificial supplement.

When the curate and the barber return to the inn, the hostess assails them for what she clearly perceives as an intimate transgression: "—Para mi santiguada, que no se ha aún de aprovechar más de mi rabo para su barba, y que me ha de volver mi cola; que anda lo de mi marido por esos suelos, que es vergüenza; digo, el peine, que solía yo colgar de mi buena cola" (339) ("By my faith, you won't take my tail for your beard any longer. You must give back my tail, for it's a shame how my husband's thing is lying about on the ground; I mean the comb, which I used to hang on my nice tail"). The double entendres proliferate bewilderingly: even as the hostess claims what is hers, she confutes the difference between *her* tail and *his* beard. More important, the removal of her tail deflates *lo de di marido:* where once it hung proudly, it now languishes shamefully. If the beard serves Don Nicolás, it deprives the innkeeper of his own masculine potency. In Judith Butler's terms, at such moments "the possibility of a failure to repeat, a de-formity, or a parodic repetition" all expose

the tenuousness of an abiding gender identity.[12] Masculinity seems both fragile and peculiarly dependent on supplements perversely controlled by wom-
en, so that the gender instability so neatly avoided by casting a sometime *doncella* as damsel at the very last minute nonetheless reappears in this insistence
on a ludicrous and undependable beard as the warrant of masculinity.

In the end Dorotea saves herself, if only by observing the rhetorical conventions of subjection to patriarchal authority. When she recognizes her seducer,
Don Fernando, at the inn, she voices her own defense much more strategically than in her first, transvestite attempt. Her appeal to Fernando highlights her
own helplessness as a seduced female and her desire to be a slave to her right-
ful master. This strategic self-abasement, which operates fully within the patriarchal code, is far more effective than the first, aborted expedition: now fate
has delivered Fernando to Dorotea, and she plays her (feminine) cards right.
But the episode involves much more than her fragile impersonation of a young
man: both the curate's and the barber's disguises, with their male-to-female
cross-dressing and ersatz beardedness, and the suggestions of racial or religious
passing in Dorotea's second, African disguise render the novel's version of
transvestism far more problematic than the simple romance trope. They hint
instead at an instability within hegemonic identities—masculinity, white Spanish Christianity—that goes far beyond the topsy-turvy but finite confusion of
romance.

In part II, Cervantes returns once again to beards and beardedness, acknowledging the staginess of romance cross-dressing even as he reworks it and complicates it in his narrative. Don Quijote's own direct involvement with transvestism occurs in the campy episode of the *dueñas barbudas* (II.36–41) (bearded
duennas), which, like the hostess's *cola*, seems to "parody the very notion of an
original" where gender identity is concerned.[13] In the Duke and Duchess's most
elaborate pageant, they have their steward and, presumably, a group of male
servants, dress up as bearded ladies who seek the knight's help after being mas-
culinized by the enchanter Malambruno. The stage is set, as it were, by the steward, dressed as the "Dueña Dolorida," who praises Sancho's goodness in terms
of beardedness ("—más luengo en bondad que la barba de Trifaldín, mi acom-
pañador" [842] ["whose goodness stretches further than the beard of Trifaldín,
my squire"]) as s/he asks for his help, to which Sancho answers with a veritable tour de force on beards: "—De que sea mi bondad, señora mía, tan larga y
grande como la barba de vuestro escudero, a mí me hace muy poco al caso;
barbada y con bigotes tenga yo mi alma cuando desta vida vaya, que es lo que
importa, que de las barbas de acá poco o nada me curo" (842) ("To say, my lady,
that my goodness is as long and large as your squire's beard means little to me.
May my soul be bearded and whiskered when I leave this life, that is what mat-

ters, and I'll not worry about the beards down here"). But beards will play a larger role in this episode than Sancho can ever imagine:

> Y luego la Dolorida y las demás dueñas alzaron los antifaces con que cubiertas venían y descubrieron los rostros, todos poblados de barbas, cuáles rubias, cuáles negras, cuáles blancas y cuáles albarrazadas, de cuya vista mostraron quedar admirados el duque y la duquesa, pasmados Don Quijote y Sancho, y atónitos todos los presentes.
>
> Y la Trifaldi prosiguió:
>
> —Desta manera nos castigó aquel follón y malintencionado de Malambruno, cubriendo la blandura y morbidez de nuestros rostros con la aspereza destas cerdas; que pluguiera al cielo que antes con su desmesurado alfanje nos hubiera derribado las testas, que no nos asombrara la luz de nuestras caras con esta borra que nos cubre; porque si entramos en cuenta, señores míos (y esto que voy a decir agora lo quisiera decir hechos mis ojos fuentes; pero la consideración de nuestra desgracia, y los mares que hasta aquí han llovido los tienen sin humor y secos como aristas, y así, lo diré sin lágrimas), digo, pues, que ¿adónde podrá ir una dueña con barbas? ¿Qué padre o qué madre se dolerá della? ¿Quién la dará ayuda? Pues aún cuando tiene la tez lisa y el rostro martirizado con mil suertes de mejunjes y mudas apenas halla quien la quiera, ¿qué hará cuando descubra hecho un bosque su rostro? ¡Oh dueñas y compañeras mías, en desdichado punto nacimos; en hora menguada nuestros padres nos engendraron! (848)

[Then the Doleful One and the other duennas raised the masks with which they had been covered and disclosed their faces, thickly covered with beards— some fair, some black, some white, some grizzled—at the sight of which the Duke and Duchess marveled, Don Quixote and Sancho were bewildered, and all the spectators were astonished.

La Trifaldi continued, "Thus did that ill-intentioned rascal Malambruno punish us, covering our smooth, soft skins with these rough bristles. Would to God he had cut off our heads with his huge scimitar instead of shading the light of our faces with this fluff that covers us, for if we think about it, my dear lords— and what I am going to say now I should say shedding fountains of tears, but the thought of our misfortune and the seas that they have already wept have dried up their humors, leaving them dry as ears of corn, and therefore I shall speak without tears—where, I ask, can a duenna go with a beard? What mother or father will pity her? Who will come to her aid? And if, even when she has a soft skin and tortures her face with a thousand concoctions and cosmetics, she can scarcely find anyone to like her, what is she to do when she finds her face a jungle? O duennas, my companions, we were born at an unfortunate time; in an evil hour did our fathers beget us!"]

Trifaldi alludes again to the romance convention of the damsel in distress who dresses in men's clothes to seek help or redress. The catch in this case, of course, is that the beards cannot be removed by the transvestites themselves to produce the anagnorisis and secure the sympathy of their "real" male saviors. In fact, the *dueñas'* beardedness (hermaphroditism, if you will) is the problem rather than the solution, and the moment of revelation comes when their *maleness* is exposed. Cross-dressing that sticks—or the beard that cannot be pulled off—undoes the convention of stage gender transformations and ironizes such easy oscillations. It also pokes fun at the medieval tradition of female saints, such as Wilgefortis (known as Librada in Spain), saved by their sudden beardedness from unwanted unions.[14] So awkward is the persistent masculinity of beardedness in this episode that the counterfeit *dueña* wishes that the enchanter had opted for removing their heads entirely. But the irony is even greater when we recall that these are *men* cross-dressing as bearded ladies and that the beards are in fact the only real or "natural" part of their appearance—a detail that Cervantes slyly alludes to by having Sancho later comment on the striking similarity between the Duke's steward (presumably still bearded) and the Dueña Dolorida (877).

The fabulous staginess of the plea to Don Quijote, with its references to the artifices of makeup practiced even by women who remain feminine, and Trifaldi's elaborate explanation for why s/he cannot actually cry at her plight (as realism would require) ironize the conventional, almost burlesque uses of transvestism as a popular draw on the stage. Much like Maese Nicolás's false beard and Dorotea's second disguise, the episode takes cross-dressing into a playful and potentially disruptive realm beyond the usual narrative conventions. Yet this stagy hyperawareness is followed soon after by its mirror opposite: an episode that explodes the conventions of romance cross-dressing by *removing* all possible traditional explanations. If the *dueñas barbudas* are an example of a romance plot that sticks, the next cross-dressing escapade disturbs the easy rationale of romance by presenting transvestism without a plot.

Island Adventures

The cross-dressing episode that proves the most resistant to any sort of explanation within the novel is the story of the children of Diego de la Llana (II.49). This "inexplicable" instance serves as a touchstone for those episodes, such as Dorotea's first disguise, that advertise the function of transvestism as a device or as a means to a heterosexual end. Diego de la Llana's two children disrupt the careful orchestration of Sancho's government of the Insula Barataria with their nocturnal excursion into new gender territory. Unlike the rest of the diversions in the Insula, their escapade is not planted by the dukes for their own amusement but presents instead an unscripted, actual disturbance of the peace and thus an unstaged moment of reflection on proper government. Before encountering the siblings, Sancho promises to cleanse his realm "de todo género de inmundicia y de gente vagabunda, holgazanes y mal entretenida" (916) (of all kinds of filth and of wanderers, lazy folk, and layabouts), yet he resolves the episode with a mild warning and a string of proverbs. Thus, while the encounter does not directly pose a challenge to the governor's authority, it immediately ironizes his aim to rid his domain of unorthodox pleasures and suggests instead that such proposed measures may be hard to enforce in any reasonable fashion.

The young woman brought to Governor Sancho has been captured by the *ronda* (patrol) while dressed as a man—and not an ordinary young man at that. The description of her clothing is highly aestheticized, almost baroque:

> Miráronla de arriba abajo, y vieron que venía con unas medias de seda encarnada, con ligas de tafetán blanco y rapacejos de oro y aljófar; los gregüescos eran verdes, de tela de oro, y una saltaembarca o ropilla de lo mesmo, suelta, debajo de la cual traía un jubón de tela finísima de oro y blanco, y los zapatos eran blancos y de hombre. (921)

> [They looked her over from top to bottom and noted that she wore red silk stockings with white taffeta garters fringed with gold and seed pearls; her breeches were green, of cloth-of-gold, with a loose jacket of the same material, under which she wore a doublet of fine white and gold stuff, and her shoes were white men's shoes.]

Through the character's elaborate masculine dress, the text directs attention to those parts of a woman's body that would normally be hidden by modesty (the main accusation against transvestite actresses on the stage) even as it eroticizes the male body that she simulates. When interrogated, the young woman describes herself as an unhappy maiden "a quien la fuerza de unos celos ha hecho romper el decoro que a la honestidad se debe" (921) (whom the spur of jealousy has driven to break the decorum that honesty requires). Thus, she introduces the romance or honor plot that often justifies transvestism elsewhere in the novel: perhaps she will prove to be another Dorotea. Yet when pressed for her story the young woman deflates the romance expectations by insisting, "—No me ha sucedido nada, ni me sacaron celos, sino sólo el deseo de ver mundo, que no se estendía a más que a ver las calles de este lugar" (924) ("Nothing has befallen me, and I was not driven out by jealousy, but simply by the desire to see the world, which in my case did not extend beyond seeing the streets of this village"). Mere curiosity, it turns out, has moved her to escape from her virtual imprisonment in her father's house by putting on her brother's clothes. She mentions specifically the allure of spectacle: bullfights, *juegos de cañas, comedias*—all of which involve the pleasure of costumes or cross-dressing (923).

But this is not the only part of the story that resists proper explanation: when the young woman narrates her adventure, we are presented with the puzzling transvestism of her brother, who, in a kind of chiasmic match, wears the clothes that she refuses:

> —Yo rogué a mi hermano que me vistiese en hábitos de hombre con uno de sus vestidos y que me sacase una noche a ver todo el pueblo, cuando nuestro padre durmiese; él, importunado de mis ruegos, condescendió con mi deseo, y poniéndome este vestido, y él vistiéndose de otro mío, que le está como nacido, porque él no tiene pelo de barba y no parece sino una doncella hermosísima, esta noche, debe de haber una hora, poco más o menos, nos salimos de casa, y guiados de nuestro mozo y desbaratado discurso, hemos rodeado todo el pueblo. (923–24)

> ["I begged my brother to dress me in men's clothes, in one of his outfits, and to take me out one night to see the whole town while our father slept. He consented to my insistent requests and dressed me in this outfit while he put on one of mine, which fitted him as though he had been born in it, because he has no trace of a beard and looks like a most beautiful damsel. An hour or so ago we slipped out of the house and, led by our young and senseless judgment, went around the entire town."]

Here, Cervantes complicates the verities of stock female-to-male cross-dressing by introducing the opposite transformation, one even more challenging to prevailing notions of proper gender hierarchies with the Spanish polity. The young man's transvestism functions as a destabilizing supplement to the (slightly) more logical escapade of his sister: she wears men's clothes to expand her confined worldview, but why is he moved to wear women's clothes? Through the chiasmic exchange Cervantes underscores the perspectivism of assigned—and arbitrary—gender roles: the young man puts on female garb in order to see differently. Yet another, more disruptive possibility involves the performance of the young man's "feminine" desire, corresponding to his sister's description of his effeminacy: lack of beard, "feminine" beauty, and so forth. While the father sleeps, patriarchal authority dissolves and the son relinquishes his heterosexual obligations as heir of his father's line in favor of an eroticized femininity. His transvestite desire—in addition to his narcissistic identification with his sister—completes the chiasmic exchange of dress, thereby destabilizing the conventional wisdom that males enjoy a greater freedom and mobility and that theirs is the privileged social role in Spanish society. The young man's choice to dress as a woman with no compulsion to do so challenges the ostensible inherent masculinity of the normative Spanish subject. The son of Diego de la Llana simply wants to experience the world as a woman. Notice that the young man owns more than one suit of clothes—his sister asks for *uno de sus vestidos*—so that his transformation, like hers, is not a strictly necessary exchange. By desiring to play female, the young man problematizes the status quo of "contained" female sexuality as the undesirable gender position; moreover, he introduces the possibility of a transvestite male desire that proves just as threatening to the prevailing gender economy.

The disruption of patriarchal authority in this kind of play underlies the transvestite daughter's account of her paternity: "—Yo, señores, soy hija de Pedro Pérez Mazorca, arrendador de las lanas deste lugar, el cual suele muchas veces ir en casa de mi padre" (921) ("I, sirs, am the daughter of Pedro Pérez Mazorca [Corncob], a wool trader in this village, who visits my father's house often"). As both the steward and Sancho note immediately, the daughter has succinctly presented two progenitors: one father who owns the house and one who goes to the house. Although the daughter admits that she is *turbada* (upset) and promptly rearranges her story (just as she will later rearrange the story of her romance motivations), the first version contains perhaps more truth than the emendation. If the phallic Pérez Mazorca (in a significant omission, the second last name soon drops out of the story) really came often to the house, such visits might explain why Diego de la Llana kept his daughter in such close confinement, in an effort to avoid a repetition of her dead mother's (possible) adultery. Yet if Mazorca were truly her father, his continued presence in Diego de la Llana's house would also serve to remind the reader that confinement does not necessarily prevent adultery, that disruptive female sexuality is difficult to contain. Hence the irony of the siblings' relative anonymity: they are never named except as the children of their father, but the certainty of that paternity is cast into doubt by the story. This muddying of the clear lines of genealogy and paternity reinforces the disruption produced by the transvestite escapade.

Governor Sancho and the Duke's steward attempt to control the disruption by, first, insisting on a clear story of paternity and, second, inscribing the two siblings into a heterosexual, nuptial model of sexuality:

—No se ha perdido nada—respondió Sancho—. Vamos, y dejaremos a vuestras mercedes en casa de su padre; quizá no los habrá echado de menos. Y de aquí en adelante no se muestren tan niños, ni tan deseosos de ver mundo; que la doncella honrada, la pierna quebrada, y en casa; y la mujer y la gallina, por andar se pierden aína, y la que es deseosa de ver, también tiene deseo de ser vista. No digo más.

... Llegaron, pues, y tirando el hermano una china a una reja, al momento bajó una criada, que los estaba esperando, y les abrió la puerta, y ellos se entraron, dejando a todos admirados así de su gentileza y hermosura como del deseo que tenían de ver mundo, de noche y sin salir del lugar; pero todo lo atribuyeron a su poca edad.

Quedó el maestresala traspasado su corazón, y propuso de luego otro día pedírsela por mujer a su padre, teniendo por cierto que no se la negaría, por ser él criado del duque, y aún a Sancho le vinieron deseos de casar al mozo con Sanchica su hija. (925)

["There's nothing lost," replied Sancho. "Come, we'll leave you at your father's house; perhaps he won't have missed you. And from now on don't be so childish or so eager to see the world, for 'the modest maid has a leg broken and stays home'; and 'The woman and the hen are ruined by roaming'; and 'She who longs to see, longs also to be seen.' I'll say no more."

... When they arrived the young man threw a pebble at a grated window and immediately a maidservant, who had been waiting for them, came down and opened the door. They went inside, leaving everyone amazed both at their charm and beauty and at their desire to see the world, at night and without leaving their town; but all this was attributed to their youth.

The steward's heart had been pierced through by love, and he decided to ask her father for her as a woman (i.e., to ask for her hand in marriage) soon, knowing that as the Duke's servant he would not be denied. And then Sancho thought of marrying the young man to his daughter, Sanchica.]

Even as the Baratarian authorities try to reorder sexuality, the siblings' gender remains impossible to pin down. Although Sancho addresses his advice to both, the proverbs he quotes have to do exclusively with the containment of *female* sexuality, as though the brother's feminine guise had stuck, making him an appropriate target for this kind of proverbial wisdom. But when Cervantes describes the siblings' return home, it is the sister who seems to disappear amid specific mentions of the brother as agent and the plural *ellos*. Yet in the following paragraph, the steward resolves to "pedírsela a su padre" (925), as though the female antecedent, and potential wife, were readily available. Clearly it is not a simple matter to restore order where there has been such play with gender roles. The proposed unions, which would establish rigid boundaries between masculinity and femininity, are never described in the novel, and the siblings' uncomplicated return home leads us to believe that the escapade will in fact be repeated.

Thus the episode of Diego de la Llana's children presents transvestism that cannot easily be dismissed as a means to an end. Even if the daughter's crossdressing were explained as an escape from the constraints of imposed femininity, her brother's transvestism seems motivated mainly by an irreducible desire to occupy a "feminine" subject position. The text's refusal to explain his crossover destabilizes the motivated instances of cross-dressing elsewhere in the novel, which ostensibly serve to restore the heterosexual order. Moreover, Sancho's tolerance of the cross-dressers within his own realm sets the stage for his subsequent encounters with another kind of passing subjects, those who more seriously challenge the borders of Spain by crossing them in altered guises.

Border Genres

I turn now from Sancho's "island" and its oddly unmotivated cross-dressing to two episodes at the end of part II where transvestism explicitly complicates the external boundaries of the nation and for which the model of what I call "epic androgyny" is most relevant. The generic play involved in moving from one model of transvestism—romance cross-dressing—to this second, more problematic epic model foregrounds the importance of literary conventions even in Cervantes's most daring representations. Such concern with genres, I conjecture, might prove a way to draw transvestism in from the margins of *Don Quijote,* to link it with such fundamental preoccupations of the novel as literary theory, the parody of popular literary forms, and the social and political satire of Counter-Reformation Spain. The challenges posed at Spain's borders by epic that passes as romance show how both genre and gender can seriously destabilize the representation of those borders.

The episode of Claudia Jerónima, the bandit's transvestite daughter (II.60), echoes Dorotea's case in a *noir* vein. It would be difficult to cast Claudia as a damsel in distress: she lives among bandits, and when she dresses in masculine attire to take revenge for a perceived offense, her costume includes a pair of pistols, a gun, and a dagger. Her style is more Amazon than page boy, and she is revealed as a woman only when she herself chooses, for the bandit leader Roque Guinart and his company fail to recognize her. Although Claudia's story includes elements from both the epic and the romance traditions of cross-dressing, the episode marks a movement toward epic's concern with the borders of the nation and religious transgressions that is prevalent in the "nueva aventura de la hermosa morisca" (II.63) (new adventure of the beautiful Morisca), which I discuss below.

One crucial element of the martial maid tradition—from Virgil's Camilla, through Ariosto's Marfisa and Bradamante, to Tasso's Clorinda and Spenser's Britomart—is a decisive androgyny that contrasts markedly with the unstable staginess of what I call "romance transvestism." If cross-dressing is occasional, contingent, and inherently unstable, then androgyny is permanent and often ends only with death. From this angle, at least, the latter appears to be the more profoundly disruptive because it represents a *continuous* destabilization of gender roles, ending only when the androgyne is killed off. In her reading of Ariosto, Valeria Finucci underestimates the challenge of androgyny by focusing excessively on ends: Bradamante's taming at the end of the *Furioso* carries more weight with Finucci than the androgyne's "seizing the phallus" through most of the text, and Marfisa's Amazon prowess, she argues, fizzles out in sororal nurturing.[15] Such critical defusing of the androgyne's role fails to consider the constraints on the epic's representation of gender trouble—perhaps reading for the end (teleological, marital, heterosexual, and phallic) is not the best way to recover the true audacity of these portrayals. One more sign of the disruptiveness of androgyny might be its relative disappearance: I conjecture that the stage popularity of romance transvestism, with its unsustainable, framed confusion, largely replaces the epic convention of androgyny, which becomes too threatening to contemplate. Yet there are elements of epic androgyny in Cervantes's text, and they address precisely the questions of transgressions at the border that these final chapters of *Don Quijote* present.

Why use martial maid figures to describe disturbing border crossings? Cervantes's strategy makes perfect sense if we consider how such figures frequently present multiple crossings—of gender, religion, "race," and nationality. Marfisa in the *Furioso* and Clorinda in the *Liberata*, to take the two most prominent examples, combine their androgyny with an uncertain religious (and therefore military) status. Marfisa's Christian origins must be revealed to her by the wizard Atlante so that she can be brought back into the fold after fighting Christians for most of the epic. But the ease with which Marfisa crosses sides—operating now according to the highly personal code of chivalry, now according to the exigencies of the moment—cannot be erased so quickly. The woman warrior remains a figure of transgression—of battle camps and religious allegiances as well gender roles.

Clorinda the Ethiopian poses an even more problematic example because of Tasso's acute concern with the religious dimension of his epic. Whereas Marfisa's character and her androgynous valor remain the same regardless of her religion, Clorinda's great moment of anagnorisis at death conjoins the discovery of her gender with her long-postponed Christian baptism as she is transformed from a Muslim warrior into the maidservant of God. Quint brilliantly shows how Clorinda's connection to Ethiopia serves to destroy the possibility of Christian heresy, if only within the epic: Christianity as practiced in schismatic Ethiopia will not do, even if such Christians might prove important allies against the Muslims.[16] But he fails to stress the connection between Clorinda's gender indeterminacy and her religious confusion: because she is a pagan on the surface, Tancredi cannot approach her other than in battle, even in those episodes where he knows she is a woman; conversely, she fights him not, primarily, because of the code of chivalry (as Marfisa might have done) but because he is on the Christian side. Finally, it is surely significant that by taming Clorinda Tasso manages to kill two birds with one stone—heresy/Islam *and* transgressive, androgynous femininity—because warrior women both condense and confound ideological binarisms.

To return to Cervantes at the border, then, consider Don Quijote's encounter with the warlike Claudia and the bandits on the way to Barcelona. The entire adventure of Claudia Jerónima occurs in a liminal space that is, by virtue of its bandit leader, imbued with more historical reality than any in the novel. Yet this authentic space exists at the expense of centralized national rule: the outskirts of Barcelona are overrun by bandits who cannot be controlled by the Catalonian viceroys. As I show in chapter 3, the *bandolers* posed a serious threat to the public order, challenging the power of the centralized state. Furthermore, as Martín de Riquer points out, Catalan bandits were often closely connected to French Huguenots—the heretics beyond the mountains—with one famous bandit known as "Lo Luterà."[17] The transgressive cross-dressing episode thus occurs within a context of liminality that recalls the constant movement between Christian and pagan camps of the warrior women in Ariosto and Tasso.

On the surface, Claudia's plight is almost identical to Dorotea's—a wayward lover has (apparently) broken his promise of marriage by taking another wife. This spurned maiden, however, takes revenge into her own hands, shooting the supposed offender and turning to a male authority figure, Roque Guinart, only for help in arranging her getaway. The resolution of the episode both insists upon the porosity of national boundaries—the frustrated Claudia intends to escape to France—and recalls the two androgynous predecessors described above: the Amazon Marfisa, and Clorinda, tragically killed by Tancredi in the *Liberata*'s most famous episode. Claudia represents both the vengeful woman warrior and the *anti*-Clorinda, as she mistakenly kills her lover and watches him die. Her outlaw justice is fatally flawed: her lover has, in fact, been faithful, and in her hasty revenge she kills him without cause, just as Tancredi killed Clorinda, who was Christian under her pagan appearance. Yet, since some kinds of justice *are* possible in the underworld, as shown by Guinart's verdicts elsewhere in these chapters, the failure of justice in Claudia's case must be attributed to something other than her outlaw existence. If her story is seen as a dark coda to Dorotea's, the message becomes quite clear: tragedy is what happens when women adopt male violence in their own defense.[18] Had Claudia cast herself as a damsel in distress rather than attacking her lover in the guise of a woman warrior, perhaps some male character would have intervened to set matters right, affording Claudia's story the same kind of resolution that characterizes Dorotea's. Instead, Claudia bows out and heads for a convent, albeit without accepting a male escort.

The case of Claudia Jerónima appears to establish certain limits to female transvestism. It recasts androgyny as an outlaw activity within a world of outlaws, a product of extreme circumstances that, if not abandoned at the earliest possible opportunity, will lead to disaster. Although Claudia retains her mobility and independence, her initiative in taking her own defense leads to tragedy. Yet Cervantes soon balances her story with another border episode that simultaneously challenges orthodox notions of gender propriety and insists upon the porosity of Spain's borders. This final cross-dressing episode, open-ended and inconclusive, explores fully the possibilities of transvestism to confound simultaneously the categories of gender, nation, and religion.

The story of Ana Félix (II.63, 65) makes transvestism a central figure for patriarchal Spain's confrontation with its own heterogeneity: all is not what it appears to be and certainly not as simple as it might seem on the surface. Cervantes titled chapter 63 "De lo mal que le avino a Sancho Panza con la visita de las galeras, y la nueva aventura de la hermosa morisca" (Of the disaster that befell Sancho Panza on his visit to the galleys, and the new adventure of the beautiful Morisca), thereby giving the cross-dressing game away but also calling attention to the significant differences between this episode and the first adventure of a beautiful Moor—the Captive's tale (I.39–41). In this later episode, the captain of the Moorish ship fighting the galley that Don Quijote and Sancho visit reveals herself to be the Christian Ana Félix, a Morisca raised in Spain but expelled by royal order. Despite the chapter's title, the interpellation of the corsair captain provides one of the most spectacular instances of anagnorisis in the novel, precisely because so many expectations and preconceptions are shattered at once. With a noose around his neck, the pirate appears "tan hermoso, tan gallardo, y tan humilde" (1033) (so beautiful, so brave, and so humble) that the viceroy is moved to ask him:

> —Dime, arráez, ¿eres turco de nación, o moro, o renegado?
> A lo cual el mozo respondió, en lengua asimesmo castellana:
> —Ni soy turco de nación, ni moro, ni renegado.
> —Pues ¿qué eres?—replicó el virrey.
> —Mujer cristiana—respondió el mancebo.
> —¿Mujer, y cristiana, y en tal traje, y en tales pasos? Más es cosa para admirarla que para creerla. (1034)

> ["Tell me, captain, are you of the Turkish nation or a Moor or a renegade?"
> To which the lad answered, in the self-same Spanish tongue, "I am neither of the Turkish nation nor a Moor nor a renegade."

"Then what are you?" countered the viceroy.

"A Christian woman," answered the young man.

"A woman and a Christian and in such an outfit and in such straits? That is a thing rather to be marveled at than to be believed."]

Here indeed is a new Clorinda whose femininity and Christianity are similarly disguised and elusive. She moves between Spain and Africa with the confidence of a true martial maid: her assumed gender affords her protection, but it is her ethnic ambiguity—she can function both in Spain and in North Africa—that allows her to pass when necessary. While Ana's story of her cruel exile into Algiers provides some background for her transformation, it by no means accounts for her disconcerting transgression of categories. The viceroy's question proffers his possible range of identities for a marauder on Spain's coast: Turk, Moor, or turncoat renegade; Ana turns his expectations on their head by revealing herself simultaneously as a transvestite and as an excluded Christian forced out of Spain into an uncomfortable allegiance with its enemies.

Ana begins her story with a lament for her "nation" (in the older sense of ethnic group): "—De aquella nación más desdichada que prudente sobre quien ha llovido estos días un mar de desgracias, nací yo, de moriscos padres engendrada" (1034) ("From that more unhappy than prudent nation, on which a sea of misfortune has recently fallen, was I born, of Morisco parents"). Yet her bewildering narrative underscores how fraught it is to connect a contemporary sense of Spain, as a newly unified nation, with older notions of ethnic nationhood. Although the Moriscos are singled out and persecuted, the difference between them and "proper" Spaniards is revealed as a fragile construct. In the multiple confusions of Ana's story, any attempt to anchor the modern nation in a non-Semitic Christian "nation" founders in the face of these Moriscos' similarity and willingness to assimilate.

When captured, Ana is ostensibly returning to Spain to search for her father's buried treasure; she specifies that she and her accomplice, a renegade "que es cristiano encubierto" (1036) (who is secretly a Christian), are to enter Spain "en hábito de cristianos, de que venimos proveídos" (1036) (in Christian attire, which we have with us). Her intended disguise rehearses the irony of Dorotea pretending to be a damsel in distress: dressed as a Christian, Ana would merely be playing what she already is. At the same time, however, her plan renders the essentialized categories of national and religious identity—the very categories, that is, according to which the Moriscos are targeted and expelled—as mere sartorial devices. In the right costume, Ana suggests, she can pass not only as man or woman but as Christian or Moor, Spaniard or foreigner. In much the same way as Sancho's old neighbor, the Morisco Ricote, who re-enters Spain disguised as a German pilgrim (II.53), Ana invokes the possibility of passing in order to remain within Spain.[19] When the disguised Ricote, on board the galley, recognizes Ana as his daughter, the marvelous, protean *arráez* is literally revealed as the girl next door. What makes her multiple transformations even more bewildering, however, is that there is no reason to doubt the authenticity of her Christian feeling: she belongs in Spain by virtue of her religion and has been expelled due solely to the ostracizing of her "nation."

Moreover, the episode conflates the difference between proper Spaniards and Spain's Others by constantly pairing Ana with an aristocratic male subject, Don Gaspar Gregorio. This Old Christian gentleman was so in love with her, Ana tells us, that he decided to follow her into exile. His own ability to pass as a Morisco by speaking forbidden Arabic enabled his departure: "—Mezclóse con los moriscos que de otros lugares salieron, porque sabía muy bien la lengua" (1035) ("He mingled with the Moriscos who were leaving from other towns because the knew the language very well").[20] The text constantly emphasizes the physical similarity between Ana and her lover—both are repeatedly described as *hermosos* and *gallardos*—as though to underscore their reciprocal ability to pass. Thus, an androgyny of sorts signals other kinds of equality and compatibility: religious, linguistic, and more generally cultural.[21] Yet when the story relocates to North Africa and the specter of sodomy is introduced, Gregorio's androgyny enables Ana to take the upper hand, a move that challenges notions of masculinist Spanish superiority even more profoundly than does their mere resemblance.

Partly because the episode focuses on an apologia for the Moriscos expelled from Spain, and partly to make other the problematic insistence of sodomitic desire, Islam abroad is reduced to a caricaturized, demonic backdrop. In her narration, Ana manipulates the degrees of difference by constantly distinguishing between Moors and Turks, with the latter consistently stereotyped as insatiable sodomites. The unsubtle representation of Islam abroad suggests that the development of the story *in* Spain merits special attention. What are the ambiguities at home that pale by comparison to the sodomy and cruelty attributed to the East?

Stephen Orgel argues that in Elizabethan England sodomy only becomes visible "when it intersects with some other behavior that is recognized as dangerous and antisocial."[22] In her comparative study of cross-dressing on the stage, Ursula Heise counters that Spain, by contrast, sees sodomy as "a transgression with features of its own": "Sodomy is not just one aspect of a general nonconformism of seditiousness, but one of the crimes most severely penalized by both inquisitorial and secular courts."[23] Yet such concreteness does not rule out the superimposition of sodomy on other types of difference. In particular, the traditional effeminization associated with the East is recast in early modern Spain, as in much of Europe, as a particular sign of Muslim sinfulness. Thus, while sodomy is understood far more specifically in Spain than in England, it is still connected in the popular Spanish imagination to various forms of otherness, notably Islam.[24]

In Ana's story, Don Gregorio is not stigmatized for his effeminate beauty, for he helplessly arouses desire in both men and women.[25] Ana exploits the uncanny resemblance between her own feminine beauty and Gregorio's to save him from the Turks' sodomitic appetites:

—Turbéme, considerando el peligro que Don Gregorio corría, porque entre aquellos bárbaros turcos en más se tiene y estima un mochacho o mancebo hermoso que una mujer, por bellísima que sea. Mandó luego el rey que le trujesen allí delante para verle, y preguntóme si era verdad lo que de aquel mozo le decían. Entonces yo, casi como prevenida del cielo, le dije que sí era; pero que le hacía saber que no era varón, sino mujer como yo, y que le suplicaba me la dejase ir a vestir en su natural traje, para que de todo en todo mostrase su belleza y con menos empacho pareciese ante su presencia. . . . Hablé con Don Gaspar, contéle el peligro que corría el mostrar ser hombre, vestíle de mora, y aquella misma tarde le truje a la presencia del rey, el cual, en viéndole, quedó admirado, y hizo disignio de guardarla para hacer presente della al Gran Señor; y por huir del peligro que en el serrallo de sus mujeres podía tener y temer de sí mismo, le mandó poner en casa de unas principales moras que la guardasen y la sirviesen, adonde le llevaron luego. (1035–36)

["I was distressed to think of the danger Don Gregorio was in, for among those barbarous Turks a beautiful boy or lad is held in greater esteem than a woman, no matter how beautiful she may be. Then the king ordered that he be brought before him so that he might see him and asked me whether what they said of that young man was true. Then, as though warned by Heaven, I said that it was but that he should know that he was not a man but a woman like myself, and I begged to be allowed to dress her in her natural costume, that she might fully display her beauty and appear before him with less embarrassment. . . . I spoke to Don Gaspar and told him the risk he ran in appearing as a man. I dressed him as a Moorish woman, and that same afternoon I brought him to the king, who, when he saw (him/her), was full of admiration and planned to save her as a present for the Great Turk. And to avoid the danger that she might be in and fear at his own hand in his women's seraglio, he ordered that (s/he) be placed in the house of some noble Moorish women who would keep her and serve her, where they then took (him/her)."]

The Turk's appetites are infinite: not only does he pose a sodomitic threat, but he cannot trust himself to respect the chastity of the "woman" that he will present to his ruler. Yet the threat of heterosexual violence against women is elided in the face of the much greater threat of sodomy. With the king focused on Don Gregorio, Ana easily protects herself from his inordinate lust by manipulating his greed, convincing him, as she tells it, to let her return to Spain for her buried treasure. Thus the appetites attributed to the Turk mask not only the "real" effeminacy of Don Gregorio but also Ana's "masculine" adventurousness (there is no indication in the story that anyone has told her to dress as a man; but her costume reflects the social role she has taken on). She plays the martial maid to perfection (recall, for example, Ariosto's Bradamante rescuing Rinaldo), while her knight waits emasculated in a feminine space. Although, as the "true" Spaniard in both ethnic and religious terms, he should clearly be the more powerful figure, he languishes instead in transvestite confinement. Ana leaves Gregorio a virtually emasculated prisoner while she takes on new adventures.

The double transvestism in this episode seems far more radical than the isolated instances of Dorotea and Claudia Jerónima. As with Diego de la Llana's two children, the *exchange* of clothing seems to complete an erotic transaction that destabilizes both gender roles, as opposed to simply pointing out the disadvantages of femininity. And, in this second captive's tale, the distraction of the Turk's far greater "perversity" shifts the focus of the narrative away from the transgressive nature of Ana's strategies. Meanwhile, she only asks for help in saving Gregorio when she is captured by the Spanish and reclaimed by her father, Ricote; it is tempting to think of her life as a Moorish pirate if her transvestite adventure had not been so rudely interrupted. When, if ever, would she have declared the adventure over? Even when Don Gregorio is finally rescued by the ambiguous figure of the renegade,[26] the text refuses to provide a complete return to the heterosexual order:

> Y aunque Don Gregorio cuando le sacaron de Argel fue con hábitos de mujer, en el barco los trocó por los de un cautivo que salió consigo; pero en cualquiera que viniera mostrara ser persona para ser codiciada, servida y estimada, porque era hermoso sobremanera, y la edad, al parecer, de diez y siete o diez y ocho años. Ricote y su hija salieron a recibirle, el padre con lágrimas y la hija con honestidad. (1046)

> [Although Don Gregorio had been taken away from Algiers in women's clothing, he exchanged it on board for that of a captive who escaped with him; but whatever dress he might have worn, he would have appeared a person to be desired, served, and esteemed, for he was extraordinarily beautiful and apparently about seventeen or eighteen years old. Ricote and his daughter went out to meet him, the father with tears and the daughter with virtue.]

Don Gregorio, the narrator implies, would incite our desires regardless of his assigned gender—his beauty dissolves traditional categories of male/female, masculine/effeminate. Clearly, the implication at his return is not that the Spaniards (those who greet him or the readers themselves) participate in the perverse desires attributed to the Turks—sodomy is what the foreigners do— yet the eroticization of his description complicates the distinction between masculine self and effeminate other. If, after he abandons the female disguise that was justified by necessity, Don Gregorio still presents the same kind of beauty, then what kind of masculinity can he possibly regain? Perhaps the experience of captivity has effeminized him (through transvestism), even if Ana has saved him from sodomy. Or is there something about his beauty that not only effeminizes him but implicates both narrator and reader in lusting after it? Is this dangerous beauty in the eye of the beholder?

Thus, in this second Moorish adventure the accusation of sodomy elsewhere comes home to roost, serving to disguise same-sex desire and the transgression of gender lines by not only Moriscas on Spain's borders but Spaniards at large. The description of his return specifies that Gregorio must exchange clothes with another liberated captive to recover his (slightly more) manly appearance. The exchange implies a chain of transvestism in which the return to normalcy becomes impossible without a new act of cross-dressing some-where. In this closed economy of dress, there will always be one man in wom-en's clothes to disturb the equilibrium. And although the connection between male transvestism and homosexuality is not always explicit, a good number of the contemporary critics of such cross-dressing link it to the "sin" of sod-omy.[27] Perhaps more significant for my argument, in theologians' writings against the theater the lassitude that comes from effeminization—whether through the theater or through ornate clothing—is connected to Spain's own vulnerability to the Moors or the English.[28] Thus, "sodomy" abroad is brought home, so to speak, in Gregorio's enduring femininity and the feminine clothes with which he has effeminized some other captive. Ana, for her part, appears similarly unwilling to return to an appropriate gender role. She does not greet Gregorio with a typically feminine show of emotion; her father cries, but her own virtue seems to consist in refraining from such displays of feeling.

Likewise, the political dimension of the plot is never resolved: now that Don Gregorio has safely been brought back to Spain, will Ana and her father be allowed to stay? After all, the entire adventure was the result of their legal ex-pulsion, and in returning they are merely passing for Spaniards. Or are they? The authorities in Barcelona are confident that a little hand-greasing will en-able them to make an exception for these highly sympathetic Moriscos, but Ricote refutes their confidence with a devastatingly ironic speech on the use-lessness of bribes and the appropriateness of the expulsion in order to rid Spain of every last trace of Moriscos who, like a *raíz escondida* (hidden root), might "brotar y echar frutos venenosos" (1047) (sprout and spread poisonous fruit). Strikingly, no one pays any attention to Ricote; the Moriscos' noble friends persist in their intent of somehow resolving his and Ana's fate at court. As the story winds to an inconclusive close, Don Gregorio expresses his sorrow at temporarily leaving Ana and the narrator reports that he did not want to leave "*doña* Ana Félix" (1047), as though to reiterate the equality between them by bestowing on her the eminently Spanish honorific. While Gregorio and their friends tend to their business, Ana stays with the wife of the Catalan noble Don Antonio, and Ricote lodges at the viceroy's (1047). And there the novel leaves them, two Moriscos comfortably ensconced in aristocratic spaces of power, firmly within Spain and eternally awaiting a resolution.[29]

Thus, in the story of Ana Félix passing disturbs the simple truths of ideology: it is one thing when Ana cross-dresses her lover to save him from the supposed sodomy of the vicious Turk and another matter altogether when both she and he fail to shed their androgyny, once back within Spain's borders, while maintaining their stubborn allegiance to each other *and* to Spain. The last episode of cross-dressing in the novel underscores not only the illusory nature of appearances but also the deceptive nature of binarisms of gender, religion, and nationality. The "Moorish" perversity exists within Spain, not only because, in the absence of an ending, Ana and her father, Ricote, seem to stay on, but because sanctioned Spanish virtues, such as the beauty of Don Gregorio or Ana's sober chastity, already have the potential to destabilize gender roles and ethnic categories regardless of the actual presence of Islam. In a sense, both the Old Christian's and the Moriscos' ability to pass—in either religious or gender terms—undermines the wholeness of Spanish identity.

Transvestism—whether practiced by beautiful young men or by warlike women at the frontier—thus works its own peculiar magic within *Don Quijote,* evincing the fragility of gender roles and masculinist, Old Christian Spanish identity. Although in the cases of isolated female transvestism traditional binarisms are restored after a momentary disturbance, the irresolution of the episodes of Diego de la Llana's cross-dressing progeny and Ana Félix and her effeminate lover provides a starting point for a reading that challenges the prevailing patriarchal modes of racialized homogeneity and masculinity in the novel. These more radical instances, especially the latter, point to the complicated intersections of gender and other categories of difference in Spain's attempt to define its geographical and ideological borders. Passing disguises not just gender but also religion or nation, while the play of genres, from trite romance to the more transgressive epic models, undoes the easy certainties of literary convention as a point of reference. Even as the theatrical immediacy of Cervantes's gender-troubling prose recalls the enduring fascination of transvestism on the Spanish stage, it demonstrates that such transformations are far from limited to that stage or, indeed, to the category of gender. Perhaps most important, by portraying a transvestite desire that links Spain and its demonized others, the episodes of transvestism transform gender into a powerful crucible for difference itself.

3

Empire Unmanned:
Gender Trouble and Genoese Gold in
"Las dos doncellas"

Much like the Ana Félix episode in *Don Quijote,* the novella "Las dos doncellas" provides a powerful example of an apparently conventional romance narrative that disguises its engagement with political and social controversies
under the cloak of transvestism. The plot features two young women who set
off on the treacherous path of the cross-dressed romance heroine to follow the
same truant lover. The ostensible conceit—beautiful wronged maidens passing as young men—is revealed in the very title of the narrative, a red herring
that suggests a tale of tame gender transgressions in the service of a marriage
plot.[1] As if the giveaway title were not enough, Cervantes immediately teases
us with the description of a mysterious lone traveler urgently undoing the
buttons of "his" tight doublet—"desabrochándose muy apriesa los botones
del pecho"—and then quickly doing them up again.[2] This introduction to the
young *caminante* (walker), with its suggestive emphasis on the ambiguous
chest/breast, conspicuously exhibits her imperfectly disguised body and announces the central role of voyeurism in the narrative. Beyond the require-
ments of an opening in medias res, the excess of information at the start—
which pre-empts a satisfying anagnorisis when the true gender of the two
travelers is disclosed—suggests that there may be more going on here than
simple romance cross-dressing. After all, if the point of the story were to tan-
talize, why not entitle it "Los dos viajeros" (The two travelers) or "Los casa-
mientos engañosos" (The deceitful marriages)?

I argue below for a symptomatic reading of the more profoundly disturbing transgressions that underlie the two damsels' transvestite quest. "Las dos

doncellas," I suggest, mounts a romance critique of epic ambitions, exposing the internal anarchy—gendered and otherwise—of a masculinist imperial Spain. By analyzing the larger repercussions of the damsels' transvestism, the historical context of Spain's fraught European empire, and the literary allusions in the narrative, I show how Cervantes challenges generic conventions in a tale of gender transgressions and how these breaches of decorum complicate the Spanish imperial project that frames the main events of the narrative.

"Las dos doncellas" was first published in 1613 as part of the collection of twelve "exemplary novellas" by Cervantes. The *Novelas ejemplares* occupy an interesting place in his oeuvre; they appeared between publication of parts I and II of *Don Quijote* (1605 and 1615, respectively) and feature a wide range of formal experimentation that both echoes and anticipates the more famous novel's problematization of genre.[3] In his prologue to the *Novelas ejemplares,* Cervantes emphasizes the originality of these tales in a Spanish context: "Yo soy el primero que he novelado en lengua castellana, que las muchas novelas que en ellas andan impresas, todas son traducidas de lenguas extranjeras, y éstas son mías propias, no imitadas ni hurtadas" (I.52) (I am the first who has written novellas in Spanish, for the many novellas now printed are all translations from foreign tongues, and these are my own, neither imitated nor stolen). Perhaps because of Cervantes's protestations of originality, critics have paid attention to the novellas that foreground realism and particularly Spanish literary innovations—such as the picaresque—while typically dismissing the more idealizing or Italianate ones.[4] As the neglected novellas have come under greater critical scrutiny, however, it is apparent that under the veil of romance they in fact address specifically Spanish social and political concerns.

"Las dos doncellas" in particular combines formal and thematic elements of the Renaissance *romanzo* of Ariosto and of medieval romance. Fleeing damsels in distress, transvestism, moral and physical wandering (*errare*), a hero diverted by love, the postponement of naming, the quest toward a deferred goal, the idealizing tone—all these suggest a clear generic identification.[5] Yet the interest of the text lies in how it transforms genre into an active and unstable category. In the first place, the text foregrounds the literary history that pits romance against epic. In its simplest form, Virgilian epic and the subsequent tradition are aligned with the public goals of nation formation, an ordered history, and the teleological exploits of a synecdochic hero, while romance signifies the derailment of the epic project—in both literary and political terms—through error, wandering voyages, and the seductiveness of female "enchantresses."[6] Historically, early modern Spain relied heavily on the *Aeneid* tradition and the conceit of *translatio imperii*—the westward progress of empire from Greece to Rome to its self-proclaimed heirs in western Europe—

to support its imperial claims.[7] This potent tradition of epic and its political versatility transform romance into a powerful vehicle of ideological critique, ideally suited to voice domestic and private objections to the costs of empire. Through his explicit thematization of the *Aeneid* in "Las dos doncellas," Cervantes harnesses what Fredric Jameson refers to as "the mediatory function" of genre in order to interrogate "the twin diachronic perspective of the history of forms and the evolution of social life."[8]

But "Las dos doncellas" goes even farther, emphasizing the instability of romance in the face of the gender disorder that the genre promotes and the disturbing moments of realism that intrude on its idealizations. If, as Anthony Cascardi argues, "the self-consciousness of romance is one of the unavoidable traces left [on Cervantes's texts] by history—whose essence is inseparable from the process of disenchantment"—in this novella history makes romance so self-conscious as to be ultimately unsustainable.[9] As romance is deconstructed, Cervantes expands his critique from the political to the literary by revealing the limitations of the very genre that enables his initial condemnation of empire.

"Las dos doncellas" begins with Teodosia's cross-dressed flight from her home in Andalucía in search of her seducer, the significantly named Marco Antonio, who has abandoned her to join the Spanish troops in Italy. Her brother, Rafael, happens upon her at an inn and hears her confession but refrains from inflicting the punishment that would salvage the family honor. Instead, he decides to escort her on her quest for redress. They learn that Marco Antonio has boarded a galley to Naples in Cádiz and decide to intercept him in Barcelona. Near the city, the two meet the cross-dressed Leocadia, who has been robbed by bandits, and are horrified to hear that she, too, is in search of Marco Antonio, having been seduced and abandoned by him, much as Teodosia was. The three nonetheless continue together to Barcelona, where the galleys put in before sailing to Italy. A phenomenal battle breaks out between the ships' crews and the townspeople, and the damsels save Marco Antonio by virtue of their swords. With the seducer wounded and on his deathbed, the marriage plot sorts itself out as Marco Antonio recognizes his greater obligation to Teodosia, while Rafael proposes to Leocadia. After Marco Antonio recovers, the four go on a pilgrimage of thanks to Santiago de Compostela before returning home in time to save their irate fathers from taking revenge on each other in a duel.

"Las dos doncellas" thus spans the length and breadth of Spain, limning a nation that transcends regional boundaries and locating it in a complex network of imperial and economic transactions on the Atlantic and the Mediterranean. From Cádiz to Barcelona to Santiago de Compostela to the unattained

Italy, the narrative maps the geographic limits of Spain while subtly pointing out its limitations as a polity. The Spain of "Las dos doncellas" is a nation embarked upon increasingly untenable imperial campaigns while plagued by internal strife—banditry, a sailors' revolt, local rivalries, battles between villagers. The characters' stories progress within a landscape of such marked disorder and with such pointed references to Spain's fraught imperial dealings that the unflappable tone of the narration becomes increasingly ironic.

Social Travesties: Justice, Lineage, Decorum

The romance plot of "Las dos doncellas" is punctuated by a set of domestic disorders that go far beyond the damsels' indiscretions. The implausible narrative is precisely situated in a topsy-turvy world, and the main point of the realism seems to be to mark the extent of the social disarray. Yet because the forward movement of the plot depends as much on these moments of realist disorder as on marvelous coincidences and see-through transvestism, the depiction of a less than ideal Spain becomes a crucial component of the narrative. As I argue below, realism frames romance in order to return us to history and to an ironic vision of imperial Spain.

The first cross-dresser, Teodosia, whose disguise is so coyly revealed to readers as the narrative begins, is further exposed through a travesty of justice. Her brother, Rafael de Villavicencio, chances upon the inn where she has just taken refuge. Desperate to see the beautiful young man who has so impressed the innkeeper and his wife—"—¿Tan lindo es, señora huéspeda?—" (202) ("Is he that good-looking, Mistress Innkeeper?")—Rafael insists on being allowed to stay in the first traveler's room: "—aunque duerma en el suelo tengo de ver hombre tan alabado—" (203) ("even if I have to sleep on the floor, I must see such a praiseworthy man"). The obliging constable who has just dined with Rafael, discussing current events such as "las guerras de Flandes y bajada del turco" (203) (the wars in Flanders and the descent of the Turk), comes up with a solution: he will knock on the door, "—diciendo que soy la justicia—" (203–4) ("saying that I am the law")—which is true enough—and that on the mayor's orders the first guest must share his room with the newcomer—a complete fabrication. Although the constable is not actually impersonating the law (the powerfully metonymic *soy la justicia* erases the distinction between the law and its agents, as well as between law and justice), he is abusing his position in order to violate the rights of the first traveler. Rafael promptly rewards his creativity with four reales, as real money buys counterfeit justice. By exposing Teodosia to her brother's eroticized scrutiny, the legal travesty enables the plot to proceed: when she reveals herself and tells the sad tale of her seduction, the young man decides to escort her on her search for her truant lover, despite the dishonor she has brought upon herself and their family. The revelation also elides the question of the homoerotic desire that impels Rafael as he forces his way into the room—a question to which I will return. The object of his intense curiosity is not, as it turns out, a beautiful young man but his own sister.

The suggestion of incest replaces that of sodomy as Teodosia fears that the young man in the other bed may be tossing and turning with an amorous passion for her:

> todavía sospechó que alguna pasión amorosa le fatigaba, y aún pensó ser ella la causa, y era de sospechar y de pensar, pues la comodidad del aposento, la soledad y la escuridad, y el saber que era mujer, no fuera mucho haber despertado en él algún mal pensamiento. (209)

> [she suspected that he was troubled by an amorous passion, and even thought that she might be the cause of it, which it was reasonable to suspect and to think, for the commodiousness of the room, the solitude and the darkness, and the knowledge that she was a woman might well have aroused some ill thought in him.]

The narrative strategy is again one of perversely knowing titillation: although the reader may well imagine that the beautiful young man is the brother Teodosia has described in her tale, the acknowledged "era de sospechar y de pensar" authorizes the imagination to run freely for the length of a paragraph or two.

Once Teodosia recognizes Rafael, she offers him a dagger with which to punish her for her trespasses in a complex zeugma that rehearses her error (*yerro*) in his phallic punishment (*hierro*): "—Toma, señor y querido hermano mío, y haz con este hierro el castigo del que he cometido—" (210) ("Take this, my lord and dear brother, and punish with this dagger the sin I have committed").[10] He refuses her offer, specifically refuting her equation of one phallic instance and the other—"por no hallar castigo igual a su locura" (210) (since he could not find a punishment equal to her folly)—and the incestuous tension is finally resolved as he forgives her and decides to help her seek redress. Despite this reprieve, however, the initial scene at the inn anticipates some of the larger disorders that Teodosia's cross-dressed expedition will reveal, disorders of an entirely different sort than her own seduction and abandonment. As the narrative progresses, her honor is safeguarded while social transgressions multiply around her.

The encounter between the two cross-dressed damsels is occasioned by a new instance of social breakdown. They first meet in a forest near Igualada (the curiously named town of "Equaled"), on the road to Barcelona. Leocadia has not had the good fortune to be discovered by a sympathetic male relative. Instead, she is introduced wearing little and tied to a tree, one of the many victims of bandits who have wreaked sartorial havoc on a group of travelers. Virtually stripped by the bandits, the travelers are an odd sight: "Era extraño espectáculo el verlos: unos, desnudos del todo; otros, vestidos con los vestidos astrosos de los bandoleros; unos, llorando de verse robados; otros, riendo de ver los extraños trajes de los otros" (213) (It was a strange spectacle to see them: some completely naked; others dressed in the bandits' rags; some weeping at being robbed; others laughing at the others' strange clothing). The emphasis on everyone's altered appearance in Igualada underscores the relation between the story's transvestism and a more general disorder. In stealing the travelers' clothes, the bandits have removed signs that locate them precisely within a social structure. Even the pronominal distinctions disappear, as the carefully balanced *unos* and *otros* collapse into *otros* and *otros* and the discrete referents are themselves equaled by a common misfortune.

Beyond foregrounding the role of clothing in maintaining social distinctions, the episode invokes the scourge of banditry in Catalonia, a reference further developed in part II of *Don Quijote*, where the knight and his squire meet the bandit leader Roque Guinart on their way to Barcelona (chaps. 50–51). So severe were the depredations of the Catalonian *bandolers* in the late sixteenth and early seventeenth centuries that they threatened the public order. As unruly agents of feuding noble houses, they challenged the power of the centralized state and the king's appointed viceroys in the region.[11] Moreover, because Barcelona served as a key conduit for bullion sent from Spain to Italy and thence to other Hapsburg possessions, the bandits also threatened the crucial link between Madrid and Spain's European empire.[12] In a sense, Catalonian banditry was the domestic equivalent of English or Moorish piracy, with spectacular robberies of Spanish bullion on the scale of Drake's plunder on the seas. But the bandits also had the heroic aura of the local rebel fighting an incompetent and willfully oblivious centralized government. In Don Quijote and Sancho's encounter with Roque Guinart, the bandit leader's generosity and sense of justice implicitly rebuke the mass hanging of bandits by the authorities.[13] Though there is no particular sympathy for them in "Los dos doncellas," Leocadia's run-in with them at Igualada reinforces the sense of a less than well-ordered Spain in which a personal journey from Andalucía to Catalonia may inadvertently cross dangerous internal boundaries.

Besides stealing everyone's clothes and money, the bandits take Leocadia's most precious possession: the marriage contract that she prudently had Marco Antonio sign when he declared his love for her. Again, the advancement of the romance plot depends on a larger institutional disorder. Whereas Teodosia's true identity is revealed through a travesty of justice, Leocadia's predicament features an authentic legal document voided by hazardous circumstance—bandits who steal that which is worthless to any but the seduced damsel. Paradoxically, in both cases the satisfying progress of the narrative depends on a hiatus of legality. If Teodosia, who has consummated her relationship to Marco Antonio, is to marry him and enact the promise of her ring, inscribed "Es Marco Antonio esposo de Teodosia" (208) (Marco Antonio is Teodosia's husband), then Leocadia's inconvenient contract—"la joya que sustentaba mi salud" (219) (the jewel that sustained my health)—must be disposed of. The ring, as romance symbol for the broken hymen, takes precedence over the legal "jewel," suggesting the greater value of an alternative, even outlaw, justice. Legality and romance justice appear hopelessly irreconcilable, much as they did when the constable played the part of *la justicia* for shady ends.

Amid all this confusion, and largely deprived of her male costume, the cross-dressed Leocadia nonetheless manages to keep her female identity hidden, at least initially. When befriended by Teodosia (still disguised as Teodoro) and Rafael, she impersonates a would-be soldier, determined to "pasar a Italia y probar ventura en el ejercicio de las armas, como muchos otros españoles acostumbraban" (214) (cross to Italy and try "his" luck in the exercise of arms, as did many other Spaniards). Duly suspicious of such expeditions, Teodosia quickly notices that the future soldier's ears are pierced. But before Teodosia can investigate further, Leocadia's story begins to unravel. When she claims to come from a town near their own, Rafael innocently asks her "cúyo hijo era" (214) (whose son she was). Bewildered, Leocadia supplies first one illustrious father, Don Enrique de Cárdenas, and then, when pressed, a second one, his brother, Don Sancho. Rafael insists that neither Cárdenas has a son, although the latter is known for his beautiful daughter. Leocadia, who is of course the daughter in question, then makes up a story of *class* impersonation to disguise her cross-dressing:

> si yo dije que era hijo de Don Enrique, fue porque me tuviésedes, señores, en algo, pues no lo soy sino de un mayordomo de Don Sancho, que ha muchos años que le sirve, y yo nací en su casa, y por cierto enojo que di a mi padre, habiéndole tomado buena cantidad de dineros, quise venirme a Italia, como os he dicho, y seguir el camino de la guerra, por quien vienen, según he visto, a hacerse ilustres aun los de escuro linaje. (215)

> [if I said I was Don Enrique's son it was so that you would consider me worthy, for I am only the son of a steward of Don Sancho's who has served him for many years, and I was born in his house, and because I angered my father, having tak-

en a large sum of money from him, I wanted to come to Italy, as I have told you, and follow the path of war by which, I have observed, even those of obscure lineage become famous.]

No soy lo que soy. The implicit social threat of the equalizing robbery is realized almost immediately: in the fiction that Leocadia spins, a humble steward's son can pass as *hijo de algo*—a noble personage—because all the travelers have been democratically stripped of their clothing. The phrase *de escuro linaje,* moreover, may refer not only to the lower classes but also to New Christians ostracized for their "unclean" blood.[14] Embedded in a larger genealogical fiction, this tale of class—or caste—transgression makes the suggestion of generalized social disarray even greater.[15] Although Leocadia's story is but a fiction within a fiction, it also reinforces the vision of Italy and the military life as a means of escape from the constraints of domestic society, a view already implicit in Marco Antonio's choice of Italy as an alternative to the marriage plot.

Teodosia/Teodoro eventually persuades Leocadia to tell the real story of her adventures by swearing on "his" honor as a knight—"por la fe de caballero que profeso" (216)—to assist and serve her. Here, false performatives replace travestied justice as the narrative pretext. The very notion of candor is qualified: the authentic confession follows a subterfuge, as it did when Teodosia was at the inn. The romance values of chivalric service to a damsel in distress prove unsustainable in a world where some knights have more than one lady and others are ladies themselves. Although, much to her dismay, Teodosia finally hears the story of Leocadia's competing claims to Marco Antonio's affections, the vexed question of the second damsel's lineage is never fully resolved. When they return home with their new husbands to find their fathers dueling, backed by "gran cantidad de gente armada, de a pie y de a caballo" (236) (a great number of armed men, on horse and on foot), Cervantes gives the name of Leocadia's father as Don Enrique, not Don Sancho (235). The transposition, which editors usually gloss as an authorial slip or even correct silently, is symptomatic of the larger disorders that mar the romance plot—ostensibly sewn up.

The general disarray is reflected not only in the adulteration of the law and legal language but also in an ironic fetishization of lineage, from the rights of a *señor y querido hermano* to the name of the father(s) to family names. At the end, the narrator becomes oddly coy about identifying his heroines, "por guardar el decoro a las dos doncellas, a quien quizás las lenguas maldicientes o neciamente escrupulosas les harán cargo de la ligereza de sus deseos y el súbito mudar de trajes" (236–37) (to guard the decorum of the two damsels, whom malicious or foolishly scrupulous tongues might charge with their light desires and sudden change of attire). But since he has already given us the names of Teodosia's brother, Leocadia's father (perhaps), and the men the two women marry, this last-minute "discretion" underscores the former damsels' transgression instead of dissimulating it. In fact, the caveat reads as a tongue-in-cheek hermeneutic prod: as "foolishly scrupulous" readers, what might we charge the text with concealing behind its conventional and tidy resolution?

Imperial Transactions

The narrator is far from coy when identifying the truant lover as "hijo de Don Leonardo Adorno" (211) (son of don Leonardo Adorno) and "un principal caballero que trae su origen de los nobles y antiguos Adornos de Génova" (217) (an illustrious knight who comes from the noble and ancient line of the Adornos of Genoa). The precise naming of the seducer, when his partners must ostensibly go unnamed for the sake of their reputations, underscores how different the consequences of an illicit affair are for men and for women. At the most basic level, his last name recalls his physical *adorn*ments, which so seduce the damsels that they abandon all discretion.[16] More important, Marco Antonio Adorno's name serves as an index of the text's concerns about the pursuit of empire.

The family name of the sometime gallant and now would-be imperial adventurer locates him as a member of the Genoese colony that had existed in Andalucía ever since the Reconquista and that traded with the Indies and the Netherlands.[17] In the late sixteenth and early seventeenth centuries, during what Fernand Braudel calls "the age of the Genoese," these merchants played a special role in Spain as moneylenders to the Crown.[18] Despite the huge amounts of bullion from the New World that enriched the royal coffers in this period, the Crown found it difficult to meet the cost of preserving its Old World empire. The war in Flanders and the depredations of English and Moorish pirates meant that imperial wealth left Spain much faster than it came in. Spain thus found itself embarked upon the pursuit of universal empire with limited and often vulnerable resources. When, in spite of the enormous quantities of silver flowing into Seville, the Crown lacked ready funds, the Genoese provided credit, becoming, as Braudel puts it, "masters of international payments, of the fortune both of Europe and of the world, the not unchallenged but well-entrenched masters of the political silver of Spain."[19] Quevedo's satirical "Poderoso caballero es Don Dinero" (Mr. Money is a powerful gentleman) neatly sums up the perceived path of wealth:

Nace en las Indias honrado
Donde el Mundo le acompaña;
Viene a morir a España
Y es en Génova enterrado.[20]

[(Don Dinero) is born honest in the Indies, where the world is with him; he comes to Spain to die and is buried in Genoa.]

Forced to borrow larger and larger sums, the Crown declared bankruptcy repeatedly, undermining the credit system on which it relied. Yet to continue the war in Flanders, Spain turned again and again to the Genoese, shipping the borrowed bullion from Barcelona to Italy, whence it would be sent by land to the restless troops.[21] The transports to Barcelona along the same route taken by Teodosia, Rafael, and Leocadia in "Las dos doncellas" were highly vulnerable to bandits, further depleting the Crown's resources.[22]

Despite bearing the brunt of the Crown's repeated bankruptcies and fulfilling an essential role, the Genoese were increasingly reviled by Spaniards as unscrupulous foreigners with too much power over the nation. Their commercial success essentially opened all doors and enabled them to marry into the noble families of Andalucía.[23] (Note that Teodosia describes Marco Antonio, the boy next door, as "más rico que mis padres y tan noble como ellos" [206] [richer than my parents and as noble as they are], while Leocadia stresses Marco Antonio's noble line but also his father's large fortune [217].) Yet by the early seventeenth century the Genoese were increasingly blamed for Spain's economic woes. Often, the animosity toward them was part and parcel of a larger critique of Spain's European empire. As Gracián puts it in his *Criticón,* "'Pues si España no hubiera tenido los desaguaderos de Flandes, las sangrías de Italia, los sumideros de Francia, las sanguijuelas de Génova, ¿no estuvieran sus ciudades enladrilladas de oro y muradas de plata?'" (If Spain had not had the drains of Flanders, the blood-lettings of Italy, the gullies of France, the leeches of Genoa, would not all her cities today be paved with gold and walled in silver?).[24]

In Catalonia, where most of the action in the novella takes place, the Genoese were particularly resented, for they had supplanted the Catalans as the great trading empire of the western Mediterranean.[25] The mercantile rivalry between Catalonia and Genoa might account for the violent, unexplained battle in "Las dos doncellas" between the galleys—under the command of a *valenciano* but probably carrying Genoese funds—and the townspeople of Barcelona. Although at the travelers' arrival the city is introduced with lavish praise, the paean is quickly undercut by a vision of civic unrest:

Admiróles el hermoso sitio de la ciudad, y la estimaron por flor de las bellas ciudades del mundo, honra de España, temor y espanto de los circunvecinos y apartados enemigos, regalo y delicia de sus moradores, amparo de los extranjeros, escuela de la caballería, ejemplo de lealtad y satisfacción de todo aquello que de una grande y famosa, rica y bien fundada ciudad puede pedir un discreto y curioso deseo.

En entrando en ella, oyeron grandísimo ruido y vieron correr gran tropel de gente con grande alboroto, y preguntando la causa de aquel ruido y movimiento les respondieron que la gente de las galeras que estaban en la playa se había revuelto y trabado con la de la ciudad. (223)

[They marveled at the lovely setting of the city and considered it the flower of the fair cities of the world, pride of Spain, terror and scourge of enemies near and far, pleasure and delight of its inhabitants, refuge for foreigners, school of chivalry, example of loyalty and purveyor of everything that a discreet and knowing desire could ask of a large and famous, rich and well-founded city.

On entering it, they heard a huge noise and saw a large crowd running with great uproar, and when they asked the reason for that noise and commotion, they were told that the people from the galleys on the beach had revolted and clashed with those of the city.]

The battle seems unexpected, to say the least, after the fulsome praise for the city. The scene evokes the idea of galley slaves up in arms, returning us to the lawlessness of banditry outside Barcelona. But the narrator informs us that such struggles were actually commonplace in the city "cuando a ella llegaban galeras" (223) (when galleys arrived there).[26]

The contemporary diarist Jeroni Pujades's description of predatory Genoese behaving like "white Moors" suggests a possible source for the turmoil:

Dit dia aprés dinar foren avisats los consellers que los de les galeres de Gènova que estavan en lo moll havian enganyada alguna gent quels feian anar a veurer les galeres y quant eran allí los ferravan al rem. Feren tancar les portes de mar y agafar a quants trobavan de las galeras. Genovesos, moros blanchs, may poden perdrer son natural.[27]

[On said day after dining the councillors were notified that those of the Genoese galleys in the port had tricked some people, making them go see the galleys and then chaining them to the oars when they were there. (The councillors) had the sea-gates closed and captured everyone they could find from the galleys. The Genoese, white Moors, can never change their nature.]

Whether or not this incident is the model for the pitched battle in "Las dos doncellas," Pujades's account underscores the tensions that plagued Spain's Mediterranean empire, given the scarcity not only of gold but also of manpower.[28] His insult seems particularly telling if we recall that the Catalonian coast, as Cervantes himself describes it in *Don Quijote* (II.63), was highly vulnerable to corsair raids in which towns were sacked and their whole populations enslaved.[29] Moreover, Pujades writes as Spain comes ever closer to expelling the Moriscos, the only Moors to remain after the fall of Granada.[30] His unflattering description of the Genoese thus suggests that transforming them into proper, generous Christians or expelling them from the body politic are the only solutions for a beleaguered Spain.

In "Las dos doncellas," the liminal battle, extraordinary yet habitual, indicates that there are other versions of Barcelona than the hyperbolically exemplary city of Cervantes's initial description. As a coastal entrepôt for bullion—and impromptu galley slaves—shipped to Italy to support an increasingly untenable empire, Barcelona marks both the limits and limitations of Spain's imperial reach. If, as I argue, Marco Antonio's presence on the galley recalls the vexed role of the Genoese as enablers of and creditors to Spain's European empire, then the pitched battle at the coast suggests how the pursuit of that empire produces internal conflict within Spain.[31] Cervantes counters this vision of disorder with the Catalan aristocrat Sancho de Cardona, who stops the melée by restraining the townspeople and who treats the Castilians with the utmost courtesy and generosity. But his behavior remains the exception in what is otherwise presented as a violent and fractured nation.[32]

While primarily resented as financial operators, the Genoese were also notorious for the seductive power of their wealth, with which they supposedly assaulted the virtue of Spanish women. As Lope puts it,

En entrando a competir
Por dama, aunque más honrada,
Ginovés, músico o cresta,
Ya entiendes, volver la espalda.[33]

[When a Genoese, a musician, or a coat of arms becomes your rival for a lady—even if she is most honest—you understand: turn your back.]

Tirso de Molina marvelously compresses the Spaniards' erotic and material insecurities vis-à-vis these rich foreigners:

Aunque vengan del Pirú
virginales intereses,
hallarlos es maravilla:
pues después que hay en Castilla
barbirrubios ginoveses,
dicen que es cosa tan rara,

que no se ha de hallar en ella
un doblón ni una doncella
por un ojo de la cara.[34]

[Although virginal assets might come from Peru, it is a marvel to find them in Castile, because now that there are blonde-bearded Genoese here, it is said that doubloons and damsels have become so rare that you cannot find one to save your life.]

In Tirso's satirical vision, once the Genoese appear on the scene Spain loses its gold as quickly as its virgins. By simultaneously seducing Teodosia and Leocadia, Marco Antonio vividly enacts the irresistibly handsome and rich foreigner.

Even more striking in this context are the financial circumstances of the damsels' escape, which underscore the material—as opposed to the moral—depredations of the gallant. When Marco Antonio leaves for Naples, the gold follows: Teodosia and Leocadia specifically mention the large sums—"cantidad de dineros en oro" (208) and "mucha cantidad de dineros" (219)—that they steal from their fathers in order to give pursuit. This seems different from the more traditional romance motif by which daughters steal from their fathers when they escape *with* their lovers, as do Zoraida in the Captive's tale in the first part of *Don Quijote* and Jessica in Shakespeare's *Merchant of Venice*. In "Las dos doncellas," there is no emphasis on filial betrayal. Instead, the damsels show a realistic concern for the material expenses of their quest—an odd concern, to say the least, in a narrative that relies so heavily on the romance mechanisms of chance and coincidence.[35] The intimate thefts of the marriage plot function, I argue, as a synecdoche for the much larger circulation of gold out of Spain and into Italy in the period. By harnessing the damsels' flight to a larger concern with the role of the Genoese in Spain, the novella can trade more freely in the currency of imperial critique. The stolen gold following Marco Antonio to Italy—a domesticated version of the huge sums that went to settle debts or to pay the Spanish soldiers fighting in Flanders—registers the text's careful calculation of the cost of empire.

Italian Affairs

The name Marco Antonio, of course, signals a very different imperial context: the battle of Actium, where the Roman Mark Antony, "with barbaric wealth and various arms," and his Egyptian lover, Cleopatra, were defeated by Octavian, soon to become the emperor Augustus.[36] When Teodosia casts herself as an abandoned Dido, denouncing her seducer, Marco Antonio, as "este segundo engañador Eneas" (207) (this second lying Aeneas), she reveals herself as a particularly canny appropriator of Virgil. Virgil presents the Aeneas who leaves Dido as a pious foil to the weak Mark Antony, feminized by Cleopatra. Teodosia's evocation of epic suggests that the desirable trajectory is not from Mark Antony to Aeneas but the inverse, from the heartlessness of the founder of Rome to the loyalty of Cleopatra's constant lover. Like Dido, Teodosia cannot countenance the hero's imperial voyage to Italy to the detriment of his pressing local obligations. In the context of vexed imperial pursuits that I describe above, her entreaty, contra Virgil, marks the novella's simultaneous alignment with romance and the domestic sphere and against the epic world of empire.

Teodosia's second comparison, of Marco Antonio to a "fementido Vireno" (207) (false Bireno), also implicitly condemns an imperial ambition that masquerades as erotic fascination. The reference is to Ariosto's dark story of Olympia, daughter of the king of Holland, in canto X of the *Furioso*. Spectacularly betrayed by Bireno, the duke of Zeeland, after she loses kin and kingdom for his sake, Olympia is an abject figure whose story suggests that imperial aspirations lead men to forget the most basic decency. Bireno defies the king of Frisia—and his newfangled weapons—to marry Olympia but soon abandons her on a desert island to pursue Frisia's daughter and yet another kingdom. Bireno's treatment of Olympia, more cruel by any measure than Aeneas's abandonment of Dido, suggests that in the age of gunpowder and inter-European rivalries, conquerors become ever more ruthless. Thus Marco Antonio, his "tiro de artillería" (207) (artillery attack) on the fortress of Teodosia's virtue concluded, moves on to Italy and other conquests. Teodosia's somewhat hyperbolic allusion to Bireno's perversity works in two ways: by analogy it condemns Marco Antonio's ingratitude to the woman who risked everything for him; by contrast it suggests that in this story erotic satiety or disillusion at home masquerade feebly as the desire for empire.[37] The paired allusions—to the pious deserter of Dido and the opportunistic traitor of Olympia—thus reinforce the sense of a romance alternative to the epic demands of imperial conquest.

Ultimately, however, the damsels' generic flexibility allows them to overturn the rules of epic as they resolve the vexed contradictions between love and empire in their favor. When the cross-dressed heroines spot Marco Antonio in the thick of the fray between galley crews and townspeople in Barcelona, they promptly join in, brandishing their swords and daggers. The page-boy deception of romance gives way to a more powerful generic model as the damsels in distress become the full-fledged martial maids of epic. Lest we have any trouble recognizing them as such, Cervantes makes their literary genealogy explicit: they are "valientes y nuevas Bradamante y Marfisa o Hipólita y Pantasilea" (224) (valiant and new Bradamante and Marfisa or Hippolyta and

Penthesilea). Whereas the Roman Mark Antony was derided for falling under Cleopatra's influence and losing his masculinity to a luxurious Africa, Marco Antonio is diminished by the contrast with the two Amazons who come to his rescue as he is felled by a most unheroic stone. The resolute Didos who set out in pursuit succeed in cutting short the imperial escapade of the "second lying Aeneas" by emulating epic models for romance ends. Thus the narrative of "Las dos doncellas" averts the epic trajectory, domesticating the would-be adventurer before he can reach Italy and delivering him to his lovers. If he began as Aeneas, he ends, appropriately, as Mark Antony. As with the latter Roman original, love triumphs over empire, although here the results are hardly catastrophic. With the marriage plot resolved, the text recuperates the adventurers (cross-dressed and otherwise) to send them on a domestic trajectory—the pilgrimage to Santiago—that replaces the imperial excursion. The pilgrimage rehearses anew the gender ambiguity of the female warriors, however, since the four young people dress in identical *hábito de peregrinos* (pilgrims' dress) all the way to Santiago and back to Andalucía, so that when she reappears Leocadia's father takes her for a man (235).[38] Despite their unusual dress, the returning children manage to reconcile their dueling fathers—two Spaniards and a Genoese. By averting an Italian expedition, they effectively pacify the domestic realm.

The romance resolution redresses Teodosia's wrongs only to replace the two damsels' martial heroism with other visions of gender indeterminacy: Rafael's claim that in marrying Leocadia he wants to be the same as her ("—determino igualarme con vos" [231] ["I am determined to become your equal"], with an echo of the fateful Igualada) and the stubbornly unisex pilgrims. What is more, the effeminization of Marco Antonio in the battle scene is not easily contained. The text insists on the convergence of gender trouble and imperial enterprise by recalling the hero's penchant for Spanish Italy as he lies wounded. The repentant seducer relates how he had decided to leave the two damsels in order to sow even more wild oats:

> hícelo con poco discurso y con juicio de mozo, como lo soy, creyendo que todas aquellas cosas eran de poca importancia, y que las podía hacer sin escrúpulo alguno, con otros pensamientos que entonces me vinieron y solicitaron lo que quería hacer, que fue venirme a Italia y emplear en ella algunos de los años de mi juventud. (229)

> [I did it thoughtlessly and with the judgment of a young man, which I am, believing that all those things were of little importance and that I could do them with no scruples, with other thoughts that came to me then and urged what I wanted to do, which was to come to Italy and spend some years of my youth there.]

Marco Antonio characterizes the pursuit of arms in Italy as the result of youthful callousness and rashness. (Recall that Leocadia, too, complicates the notion of Italian soldiering when she makes up the story of her own expedition to disguise her pursuit of Marco Antonio.) In the world of the novella, a number of disparate excursions pass as the pursuit of empire.[39]

While Italy, as part of the beleaguered Hapsburg Empire in Europe, is a fine destination for a Spanish adventurer, it has an alternative set of cultural connotations that complicate a strongly masculinist reading, connotations perhaps obliquely implied by Marco Antonio's mention of other thoughts and other urges. The constant referrals to Italy as the alternative to marriage in a narrative that titillates the reader with its display of beautiful lads, whether actual young men or cross-dressed women, suggest the common association in the period between Italy and sodomy.[40] While Italy represented luxury and vice more generally, the connection with sodomy was so established that *lo de Italia* (the habit of Italy) was a common euphemism at the time.[41] In the popular imagination, *el pecado nefando* (the unspeakable sin) and effeminacy were not considered the exclusive prerogative of Italians, however, but also characterized those who had simply spent time in Italy.[42] Much as in early modern England, sodomy in Spain was consistently associated with a nefarious other, whether Italian, French, Moor, Turk, or American native. Italy posed a special threat because of the constant traffic between the metropolis and its more perverse imperial possessions. When the viceroy's Italian cook was convicted for sodomy in Barcelona, Pujades bemoaned the "'mala casta italiana quens ve a inficionar del que glòria a Déu està neta Catalunya'" (evil Italian caste that comes to infect us with that of which, God be praised, Catalonia is clean).[43] Italian mores, it was feared, could contaminate Spaniards in their own land, whether or not they had sojourned in Italy.

Marco Antonio's attempted escape from his redoubled heterosexual obligations into a life of soldiering is thus even more equivocal than might at first appear. With Italy as both imperial theater and sodomitic playground, the pursuit of empire, which Teodosia so bemoans, is put in a new light. While Marco Antonio never reaches Italy, his Italian preoccupation seems to color many of the events in the domestic realm. With Rafael and the two cross-dressed damsels, he inhabits a Spain rife with the voyeuristic pleasures of watching young men who might or might not be women in disguise. The narrative stages an abundance of erotically ambiguous scenes, from the initial display of the beautiful traveler out of breath, to Rafael's insistence on beholding "him" at the inn, to the general fascination as the wounded Marco Antonio embraces the self-same "pageboy" (230). The "habit of Italy" seems everywhere in Spain as the damsels take to male habit. Their generically routine cross-dressing makes Spanish masculinity oddly fungible. On the one hand, the characters' femaleness behind the disguise neutralizes the scenes of same-sex desire. On the other hand, the bewildering interchangeability as women occupy the place of men whom other men desire renders gender distinctions and erotic interdictions largely irrelevant. The damsels' almost routine transvestism to achieve heterosexual ends enables the staging of far more disruptive erotic possibilities within Spain, while the hero and husband-to-be longs for Italy.

To what extent can the damsels' cross-dressing express a larger critique of masculinist epic expansion? Does a Genoese Spaniard's narrowly averted adventure to Naples suggest that Italians have themselves colonized a Spain of unsettled borders, huge debts, and erotic ambiguity? With its complex apparatus of historical and literary allusion, "Las dos doncellas" unmans empire in multiple ways. The apparent resolution of the plot, which naturalizes Marco Antonio as Spanish, suggests a clear and ultimately manageable criticism of empire: save the men and the gold for Spain; do not enlist, but attend instead to your domestic obligations and go on pilgrimage. At a more profound level, however, the damsels turned Amazons and the Italian proclivities within suggest that Spain's prolonged imperial endeavors have fundamentally unmanned the nation, introducing a larger social disorder that cannot be contained by a successful romance resolution. The damsels' challenge not only to generic decorum but also to the more general strictures of gender exceeds the limits of the marriage plot. As they pass, they leave in their wake theft, prurient voyeurism, impersonation, lies, false paternity, pitched battles—a landscape of general disarray that is not addressed by the forceful summoning of Marco Antonio to his obligations. This more extensive vision of disorder cannot be contained by the resolution of the double marriage plot but remains even when the damsels presumably return to female dress and Marco Antonio sagely abandons his imperial vocation for the domestic sphere. Despite the apparent resolution, romance itself has been exposed as an unstable category, vulnerable to the intrusions of historical realism and to gender disorders. The generic and gendered transvestism of "Las dos doncellas" unmans Spain long after the protagonists have resumed their proper attire.

Passing Pleasures:
Costume and Custom in "El amante liberal" and *La gran sultana*

While Cervantes's "Las dos doncellas" examines the gender economy of peninsular Spain and the enervating cost of its empire, both "El amante liberal"—another of the *Novelas ejemplares*—and the play *La gran sultana Doña Catalina de Oviedo* catalog the cultural and religious transactions of Spanish subjects at the frontier of Christendom. Set in the eastern Mediterranean of Sicily and Cyprus against the backdrop of the Turkish threat, "El amante liberal" focuses on the far reaches of Spain's empire at a liminal time and place; *La gran sultana,* meanwhile, locates an Old Christian woman at the very heart of the Ottoman Empire. Both texts transfer the peninsular opposition between Spaniards and Moors to a more exotic and fluid version of Christian selves versus Muslim others, eschewing the North African stages more familiar to Spaniards in favor of an Eastern world in which the certainties of Spanish ideology are cast into question. The thinly veiled relativism of these two texts betrays a high regard for Turkish strengths even as their emphasis on the pleasures of passing charts the fragility of the border between Christendom and Islam, masculinity and effeminacy.

The plot of "El amante liberal" follows corsairs, renegades, and captives along the contact zone between Christianity and Islam—Cyprus, Malta, Pantelleria, Trípol de Berbería, Palermo, Messina—mapping the geography of the Mediterranean in-between. Ricardo, a Sicilian captive, tells the renegade Mahamut of his love for the beautiful but disdainful Leonisa, who prefers Cornelio, a delicate, effeminate lad. Ricardo confesses that, overcome by passion, he attacked Cornelio in a coastal garden, causing Leonisa to faint and Cornelio to flee, at the precise moment that Turkish corsairs raided the town, capturing both the spurned lover and his beloved. The pirate captain, captivated by Leonisa, decided to "turn her Moor" and marry her, but his plan was foiled by a storm and shipwreck. Once in Cyprus, Ricardo fears Leonisa has drowned, but she reappears, captive and exquisitely dressed as a Moor, almost as soon as he has finished narrating her untimely death. The Turkish "viceroys," Hazán and Alí Bajá, fight over Leonisa until the *cadí* intervenes, announcing that he will take her to the sultan's harem, in Constantinople, as a present. Aided by Ricardo and Mahamut, who have their own plans for the voyage, the *cadí* secretly hopes to claim that Leonisa has died in transit, kill his wife, Halima, instead, and keep Leonisa for himself. The captives see their chance when the ship is attacked by Christians. Are these Christian pirates from Malta? they wonder hopefully. In fact, the raiders are Hazán's Turks in disguise, passing to hide their treachery as they attempt to kidnap Leonisa. False Christians attack the real Turks, and the real Christians escape, traveling to Sicily with the renegades, who have decided to return to Christianity.

As this brief summary suggests, despite the novella's reliance on storms, shipwrecks, and miraculous coincidences, it charts a very precise geography of intense engagement between two cultures. The deliberate and carefully rendered realism of the setting qualifies the Byzantine plot; as in "Las dos doncellas," the interplay of generic convention and historical realism enables a particular kind of narrative irony.[1] "El amante liberal" engages with pressing issues of identity and empire while passing as a fantasia on Byzantine themes.[2] The narrative does more than simply challenge the absolute distinctions between Christians and Turks by stressing the porosity of borders in the eastern Mediterranean; it also mounts a critique of Spanish empire *in disguise* by transforming the trope of cross-cultural transvestism into a powerful ironic device. The characters' more or less conventional impersonations prepare the reader for the ironic interchangeability on which that critique depends: if a Christian can pass for Turk or a Turk for Christian, then attacks on the Turks may just as easily disguise attacks on Christian—and, more specifically, Spanish—practices.

But surely "El amante liberal," the only one of the *Novelas ejemplares* that is neither set in Spain nor features any Spaniards among its main characters, cannot be a reflection on Spain? In fact, the imperial critique is only reinforced by the apparent remoteness and exoticism of the setting. It is well established that for English writers and audiences of the period, as Andreas Mahler points out, an Italian setting "opens up the possibility of covert thematisation of indigenous problems," with "stage Italies" as "imaginary complements to the complex realities of early modern England."[3] The mirroring effects are even more complex in the case of Spain. In chapter 3 I suggest how Spanish anxieties about sodomy are "exported" to Italy by attributing to Italians what is *nefandum*—unspoken, if not unheard of—in Spain and how "Genoa" references the endless expense of maintaining the empire. Spain's own Italian possessions become particularly significant settings, I would suggest: close enough to reflect the metropolitan self, yet strikingly different in some respects.

Sicily, like Naples, was for centuries part of the Aragonese Mediterranean Empire before it became a Hapsburg possession.[4] In the sixteenth century it functioned as a frontier province—a bulwark against the Turk.[5] To depict Sicily and Sicilians is thus, at one level, to depict the Spanish imperial self at the margins. Much as in English texts, Italy functions as both stand-in for and alternative to the locus of cultural production. Yet the density of cultural connections that attend Spain's imperial presence in Italy make the comparisons especially complex. While the empire is metonymically invoked through the representation of its colony, Sicily's position as imperial outpost significantly complicates the representation of Turkish rapacity: the contested space here is not only a vulnerable edge of the empire but also an outlying possession with a long history of both Islamic and Christian domination and, consequently, a more fluid identity. Although "El amante liberal" features Sicilians rather than Spaniards interacting with the Turks, it nonetheless voices a powerful critique of the metropolis and its conceptual, as well as its physical, borders.

Crossing the Line: Invasion, Apostasy, Costume

Recent interpretations of "El amante liberal" have noted the conflation of religious difference in the narrative. Paul Julian Smith, William Clamurro, and Miguel Angel Vázquez all underscore the significance of the renegade as a figure who transcends the differences between Christianity and Islam and disturbs the ideological certainties of a narrative of captivity.[6] Edwin Williamson, reading in a different vein, suggests that the novella's subtext brings together ethics and aesthetics to subvert "binary structure and simplistic patriotism."[7] In fact, the novella is dense with all kinds of crossovers, from territorial invasion to religious indeterminacy to the sartorial pleasure of dressing as the other. As Carroll B. Johnson points out in his superb materialist reading of the novella, "It seems that all the official dividing lines of antagonistic religions, ethnicities, national sovereignties, and international rivalries are systematically undercut by a close-knit, mutually interdependent economic system manned by individuals with ties on both sides of the divide, and who come and go in the pursuit of ends that transcend the official differences. The normal categories of identity become less and less relevant."[8]

The tale begins in medias res with Ricardo weeping for the capital of Cyprus, the Venetian outpost conquered by the Turks in 1570: "—¡Oh lamentables ruinas de la desdichada Nicosia!" (137) ("Oh, lamentable ruins of unhappy Nicosia!"). The precise setting has the odd edginess of an old headline: it marks in great detail the temporary and unstable boundary of Ottoman encroachment in the eastern Mediterranean. As if to belie Ricardo's fresh sorrow, the bulk of the action and his embedded narrative of previous woes are set at the moment when one *bajá*, or governor, of Nicosia takes over from his predecessor, suggesting that Turkish control has solidified enough for the institutions and traditions of government to take their place (140–41).

The Ottoman conquest of Cyprus marks a dark moment in Christianity's struggle with Islam. While the war in Flanders, naval skirmishes with England, and the Morisco uprising in Granada strained Philip II's resources, it was feared that Turks and Moors might join forces to take Spain itself. With Spain otherwise engaged, Cyprus fell to the Turks a scant year before the battle of Lepanto, "donde quedó el orgullo y soberbia otomana quebrantada" (I.39) (where the Ottoman pride and haughtiness were broken), as the Captive puts it in *Don Quijote*.[9] The temporal proximity of the great Christian defeat to the great victory that followed makes the setting of the novella particularly intriguing. Given that the Turks have controlled Cyprus for two years when the story opens, the absence of any reference to Lepanto is striking, especially since Cervantes makes much of his own role in the battle, and his honorable wound, in the prologue to the *Novelas* (51). The reticence suggests that the great victory of the Holy League in October 1571 has changed very little. The transformation of Christian outposts into Ottoman footholds, the corsair raids, and the concomitant metamorphoses of Christian subjects into exiles, captives, or renegades continue despite Juan de Austria's stunning triumph. Cyprus remains in Turkish hands, a sorry sight for Christians and even for a sympathetic Turk:

—Bien tendrás que llorar—replicó el turco—, si en esas contemplaciones entras; porque los que vieron habrá dos años a esta nombrada y rica isla de Chipre en su tranquilidad y sosiego, gozando sus moradores en ella de todo aquello que la felicidad humana puede conceder a los hombres, y ahora los ve o contempla, o desterrados della o en ella cautivos y miserables, ¿cómo podrá dejar de no dolerse de su calamidad y desventura? (138)

["You may well weep," replied the Turk, "if you enter upon those contemplations, for those who some two years ago saw this renowned and wealthy island of Cyprus in its peace and quiet, with its inhabitants enjoying everything that human happiness can grant, and sees or contemplates them now, either banished from it or captive and miserable upon it—how could one not lament their calamity and misfortune?"][10]

Even more striking than the vision of instability in this passage is the fact that it is spoken by a "Turk," Mahamut. Already the narrative suggests that appearances may be deceiving and that the violent oscillation between happiness and misfortune, between Christianity and Islam, may include many intermediate positions. While the *bajás* who are the primary antagonists in the narrative are themselves renegades of Italian origin—the historical Alí Pasha, a Calabrian, and Hasán Pasha, a Venetian[11]—their hybridity is presented with unremarked irony while Mahamut's divided allegiances become central to the narrative.

The conflation of difference continues as Mahamut begs Ricardo for his story, "por lo que te obliga el ser entrambos de una misma patria, y habernos criado en nuestra niñez juntos" (138–39) (as you are obliged to by our being from the same native land and having been brought up together in our childhood). The Turk is thus revealed as a renegade, although the exact circumstances of his apostasy are never clarified. Ironically, despite the fact that the main antagonists are also Italians, Mahamut's claim of Sicilian origins here ostensibly serves to explain the positive initial description of him as a Turk "de muy buena disposición y gallardía" (good-looking and brave) whose first words are, "—*Apostaría* yo, Ricardo amigo" (138, my emphasis) ("I would bet, friend Ricardo"). The linguistic echo of apostasy here coexists with Mahamut's claim on Ricardo's friendship, which the latter never questions, despite the renegade's present condition.[12] The friendship is in fact fully reciprocated: the Turk becomes "—¡oh Mahamut hermano!" (154) ("Oh, brother Mahamut") as Ricardo finishes his tale of woe. Thus the entire embedded narrative, which takes up almost a third of the novella, is presented under the aegis of obligation to a Turk who, paradoxically, can claim to be the Christian's compatriot.

The frame for Ricardo's tale substantively undermines any sense of essential enmity between Turks and Christians, for the very condition of the telling is the hero's connection to a sympathetic other much like the Christian self. Mahamut's matter-of-fact claim that there must be something wrong with Ricardo (beyond his present confinement, since he has ample resources with which to ransom himself) relativizes the perils of captivity that the renegade himself has earlier lamented and diverts the focus of the narrative. Moreover, the renegade's central role in both exposition and resolution suggests that the narrative depends on the imaginative power of allegiances that cross the Islamic-Christian divide. Mahamut remains, throughout the novella, one of the most sympathetic and reliable renegades in the entire literature of captivity, despite his rather attenuated Christian leanings.

The benign vision of the renegade in "El amante liberal" is compounded by the striking fluidity between Christianity and Islam. Halima, smitten with Ricardo, decides to follow him *a tierra de cristianos* (to the land of the Christians), to the delight of her Christian Greek parents (181).[13] She and Mahamut are summarily reconciled to the Church, and, since Ricardo is otherwise engaged, she contents herself with marrying his friend. The conventional romance ending, with the second couple amicably and pragmatically pairing off, calls attention to the surprising simplicity of the conversion, which shares with the marriage one very eventful sentence: "Reconciliáronse con la Iglesia, Mahamut y Halima, la cual imposibilitada de cumplir el deseo de verse esposa de Ricardo, se contentó con serlo de Mahamut" (187–88) (Mahamut and Halima were reconciled with the Church, and she, unable to fulfill her desire to become Ricardo's wife, was content to be Mahamut's). The transition to Christianity is both straightforward and oddly unmotivated, much like Halima's sudden affection for Mahamut. He has not alluded to his religious fault since early in the narrative, while Halima never voices any Christian feelings. There is no protestation of true faith, no formal examination by the Inquisition, simply a reconciliation as facile as the romance dénouement. Only the slight vacillation as to which Church authority is in charge of the process—the text hesitates between the "obispo o arzobispo de la ciudad" (187) (bishop or archbishop of the city)—suggests the unorthodoxy of these proceedings.[14]

The novella's vision of Sicilian openness—no questions asked at repatriation—contrasts markedly with Cervantine texts that dwell on the complexities of admitting into Spain those who express a desire to (re)turn Christian.[15] In the Captive's tale in the first part of *Don Quijote,* for example, Zoraida refers constantly to her Christian faith; her transformation could not appear more irreproachably motivated, yet she protests so much that critics have been left to wonder what lies beneath such insistent claims of religious longing.[16] Zoraida lands surreptitiously yet appears, thanks to her limitless devotion to the Virgin, to find a place for herself in Spain.[17] However, the renegade who accompanies her and the Captive must go to Granada and face the Inquisition in order to rejoin the Church. Zoraida's insistent claims of Christian faith are echoed in the case of Zara, in the main plot of *Los baños de Argel*—a simpler version of "The Captive's Tale." In that play, the renegade Hazén, who intends to return to Christianity and to Spain, must collect signatures from Christian captives who will vouch for his sincerity. Despite these testimonies, the text denies Hazén his "promised land" as he dies violently in Algiers. The expulsion of Ricote and Ana Félix, which I discuss in chapter 2, hews most closely to the historical reality of early seventeenth-century Spain: Moriscos are not welcome, whatever their religion, and all New Christians are suspect. Thus the openness of a Sicily that welcomes one and all contrasts quite markedly with the closed Spain that Cervantes describes elsewhere.

The porosity between Christianity and Islam in the eastern Mediterranean emerges most clearly in the bewildering promiscuity of costume in the novella. Christians dress as Turks and Turks as Christians for aesthetic as well as strategic reasons. The first instance of ethnic cross-dressing is the *hábito berberisco* (Moorish garb) that Leonisa wears when she appears in Cyprus as a captive commodity.[18] The elaborate costume provided by her Jewish owner becomes a central part of the cultural and commercial transactions of the text, enhancing her aesthetic and her exchange values. The detailed description of her dress involves both narrator and reader in the voyeuristic consumption of her beauty; what makes Leonisa more appealing to her potential Turkish buyers also increases the readerly pleasure:

> traía de la mano a una mujer vestida en hábito berberisco, tan bien aderezada y compuesta, que no lo pudiera estar tan bien la más rica mora de Fez ni de Marruecos, que en aderezarse llevan la ventaja a todas las africanas, aunque entren las de Argel con sus perlas tantas. Venía cubierto el rostro con tafetán carmesí, por las gargantas de los pies que se descubrían, parecían dos carcajes, que así se llaman las manillas en arábigo, al parecer de puro oro; y en los brazos, que asimismo por una camisa de cendal delgado se descubrían o traslucían, traía otros carcajes de oro sembrados de muchas perlas. (157)

> [he led by the hand a woman dressed in Moorish garb, so well adorned and bejewelled that not even the richest Moorish woman of Fez or Morocco could equal her, even though they surpass all other Africans in adorning themselves, even those of Algiers with all their pearls. Her face was veiled with crimson tafetta; around her ankles, which were just visible, two *carcajes*, as bracelets are called in Arabic, appeared, seemingly of pure gold; and on her arms, which were similarly just visible or translucent through a blouse of the thinnest silk, she wore other gold *carcajes* studded with pearls.]

The description literalizes Ricardo's earlier evocation of Leonisa's beauty: his Petrarchan blazon—hair of gold, teeth like pearls (142)—is deconstructed in this artificial *mora,* whose bejewelled body upends the conventions of love poetry. Leonisa's body parts are scrambled and confused with the jewelry she wears, calling attention to the artifice of the entire production: on the *gargantas* (literally, "throats") of her feet she wears *manillas* (literally, "little hands"). With its echo of Petrarchism and its fetishistic pleasure in its own richness, the passage participates—and invites the reader to participate—in a commodification of women that is otherwise ascribed to Turkish captors.[19]

The text explicitly conflates Leonisa's worth with that of her Moorish costume. In a rare aside—"y así era la verdad" (160) (and that was the truth)—the narrator acknowledges that the rich costume is worth half again as much as Leonisa herself. And yet it cannot readily be distinguished from her: the rows of pearls in her tresses "con extremada gracia se enredaban con ellos" (160) (were entangled with them with utmost grace). The fetishized captive is one with her Moorish garb, and all agree that she must be sent to the sultan in her exquisite costume. Far from scandalizing anyone, her appearance gives enormous pleasure to Turks and non-Turks alike. Part of the frisson lies in seeing through: literally, through the thin silk of Leonisa's dress, but also metaphorically, through her Oriental garb. She bests the most beautiful Moor of Fez or Morocco, but she is also, despite Mahamut's failure to recognize her, clearly not a Moor. The voyeuristic delight stems from a pellucid cultural transvestism that only enhances her beauty.

Ricardo, although distraught "de ver andar en almoneda su alma" (160) (to see his soul up for auction), shares with Mahamut a similar episode about a Moorish blonde, related to him by his father, who served the emperor Charles V "en honrosos cargos de la guerra" (164) (in honorable military positions). The imperial interlude in the text underscores the parallelism between Spaniards and Sicilians as Hapsburg subjects—thus a Sicilian can recount his father's experiences on the imperial battlefront. But the interpolated narrative also sets up more complex analogies, rehearsing the auction scene with a very different cast. Here, the most explicit consumer of female beauty is Charles V on his conquest of Tunis, while the golden-haired beauty is an actual Moor. Ricardo notes the singularity of this figure: "los cabellos de la mora . . . con los mismos del sol en ser rubios competían, cosa nueva en las moras que siempre se precian de tenerlos negros" (164) (her hair rivaled the sun itself in its blond color—a new thing in Moorish women, who are always proud of having black hair).[20] Whereas in the initial episode the Turks are most visibly seduced by Leonisa as Moor, in this odd replay the emperor and two of his Spanish gentlemen, one Andalusian and one Catalan, respond to the beauty of a blonde Moorish woman.

The scene challenges the apparent distinctions between Christianity and Islam at two different levels: first, through the Moor's European appearance, which suggests the existence of whole classes of in-between subjects—Moors who can pass, assimilated captives, renegades—and second, through the structural equivalence of the Spaniards to the Turks of the main narrative.[21] As if to emphasize the crossovers, Mahamut interrupts Ricardo's enraptured comparison of Leonisa's recent appearance to the Tunisian episode with a brusque "—detente, amigo Ricardo, que a cada paso temo que has de pasar tanto la raya en las alabanzas de tu bella Leonisa que, dejando de parecer cristiano, parezcas gentil" (164–65) ("say no more, friend Ricardo, for with every step I fear that you will so cross the line in praise of your beautiful Leonisa that you will cease to seem Christian and seem pagan instead").[22] Such advice from a renegade must surely be ironic, yet it establishes the connection among Leonisa's temporary sartorial transformation, the viewers' pleasure in that transformation, and the erasure of more profound religious differences.

The representation of the erotic as a means to transcend the Islamic/Christian divide was, of course, highly conventional in sixteenth-century Spain.[23] What is different here is the recurrence of a Turkish scene with Spanish protagonists and the emphasis, in both cases, on a paradoxical blonde Moor. Moreover, the protagonism of the soldier-poets in the second scene suggests a more deliberate commentary on literature and empire than in traditional representations of noble Moors and their beautiful ladies. The text stresses the Spaniards' interdependence as they collaborate on a poem to the golden-haired Aja: when one poet is unable to finish his improvised *coplas,* the other assists him.[24] Their perfect complementarity suggests the union of Castile and Aragon, evoked here by their Andalusian and Catalan identities.[25] But whereas that union—arguably the birth of modern Spain—is generally associated with territorial consolidation and the defeat of the Moors in Granada, these representatives of the new Spain sing of their own erotic defeat in Tunis. The *coplas* on which the poets collaborate rewrite Charles's victory into a defeat at Muslim hands:

> Como cuando el sol asoma
> por una montaña baja,
> y de súpito nos toma,
> y con su vista nos doma
> nuestra vista, y la relaja;
> como la piedra balaja
> que no consiente carcoma,
> tal es tu rostro, Aja,
> dura lanza de Mahoma,
> que las mis entrañas raja. (165)

[Like the sun, which, when it peers over a low mountain, takes us unawares and with its sight tames and disarms our sight; like the beryl, which resists all decay; so is your countenance, Aja, a hard lance of Mohammed that tears my entrails apart.][26]

The Petrarchan conceit of erotic violence is here refigured in terms of the struggle between Christianity and Islam. The golden-haired Aja, whose very name suggests humiliation or linguistic violence (*ajar* [Sp.] means to mistreat or abuse), tames Spaniards with her sight. More striking, her face becomes a masculine "hard lance of Mohammed" that tears them apart. The *coplas* thus reverse the Spanish triumph, as the soldier-poets construct a rhetorical defeat precisely couched in martial terms. At the heart of Ricardo's recollection of the imperial victory lies a poem that calls into question the certainties of Spanish ideology by praising the phallic beauty of a blonde Moor who vanquishes Spanish warriors. One could, of course, argue that it is precisely the defeat of the Moors that defuses the image and makes it available for Petrarchan improvisation; but, in fact, by the time Cervantes wrote his novella Tunis was long lost, reconquered by the Turks in 1574.[27] The poem thus becomes one more marker of the oscillation between Christianity and Islam in the contact zone as it looks ahead to Spanish defeats, veiling them in the language of erotic fascination.

To complicate things even further, the poem's specific mention of Mahoma's lance recalls the renegade Mahamut (a variant of the Prophet's name), as if to underscore the confusion of friend and foe in the narrative. Mahamut is emphatically (and conveniently) uninterested in erotic conquest: he is the only one who seems indifferent to Leonisa and marries Halima simply to achieve a proper romance ending. Yet here his name—unremarked elsewhere—is associated with the most militant vision of Islam. Up to this point the narrative has effectively avoided the question of what Mahoma/Mahamut is doing on the side of a Christian captive; now it challenges the reader's complacency by underscoring the duplicity of the renegade's position.

The novella stages two more scenes of cultural transvestism—one highly conventional, the other completely mystifying. When Hazán Bajá's Turks attack the Cadí's ship *a la cristianesca* (in Christian guise), their disguise is almost overdetermined: they are engaging in the familiar corsair strategy (one practiced by Europeans as well as North Africans) of disarming the enemy by disguising their true colors. More specifically, they need to hide their identity from the *cadí*, whom they are betraying in order to kidnap Leonisa. Close up, however, the disguise does not work: the disguised Turks are interpellated "en lengua turquesca" (179) (in the Turkish tongue) and give themselves away. The *cadí*'s reproach to the traitor recalls the ambiguity of Mahoma/Mahamut discussed above: "—¡Oh cruel renegado, enemigo de mi profeta! . . . ¿Cómo, maldito, has osado poner las manos y las armas en tu cadí, y en un ministro de Mahoma?" (180) ("Oh cruel renegade, enemy of my prophet! . . . How have you dared, oh cursed one, to raise your hands and your weapons against your *cadí*, a minister of Mohammed?"). There are renegades and traitors on both sides, the *cadí* reminds us: what is a fortunate betrayal for the Christians is a disaster for the Turks. Ricardo and Leonisa's reliance on Mahamut is complicated by the insistence here on the enormity of betrayal. Moreover, as Paul Julian Smith indicates, it is not only Mahamut who is skilled in duplicity: the Christians in captivity prove "more adept at deception than the Turks themselves, who are (we are told) naturally mendacious."[28] Edwin Williamson qualifies the Christians' duplicity by pointing out that they themselves allude to the moral dangers of their role-playing.[29] Ricardo recognizes that a greater danger calls for him to lose "el derecho que debo a *ser quien soy*" (170, my emphasis) (the right that I owe to being who I am) and reluctantly agrees to the necessary deceptions.

But the end of the novella presents an instance of sartorial deception so completely unmotivated as to throw into question Ricardo's attachment to an essential self. In a striking contrast with the overdetermined Turks *a la cristianesca*, the liberated Christian captives adopt Turkish disguise for no readily apparent reason beyond *una graciosa burla* (an amusing trick). After decorating the ship with colorful silks, Ricardo rehearses the commodification of Leonisa in her Moorish finery; then he proceeds to involve everyone on board in the deception, even when they must peel their disguises off the backs of their dead enemies:

> En este entretanto había Ricardo pedido y suplicado a Leonisa que se adornase y vistiese de la misma manera que cuando entró en la tienda de los bajaes, porque quería hacer una graciosa burla a sus padres. Hízolo así, y añadiendo galas a galas, perlas a perlas, y belleza a belleza, que suele acrecentarse con el contento, se vistió de modo que de nuevo causó admiración y maravilla. Vistióse asimismo Ricardo a la turquesca, y lo mismo hizo Mahamut y todos los cristianos del remo, que para todos hubo en los vestidos de los turcos muertos. (183–84)

> [In the meantime Ricardo had entreated and begged Leonisa to adorn and dress herself in the same manner as when she had entered the pashas' tent, because he wanted to play an amusing trick on her parents. This she did, and adding finery to finery, pearls to pearls, and beauty to beauty, which happiness often enhances, she dressed herself so that she again caused admiration and wonder. Ricardo likewise dressed in the Turkish fashion, as did Mahamut and all the Christians at oars, for there were enough clothes for them all among the dead Turks.]

What perverse pleasures does this joke provide? At one level, the scene reads as a metaliterary reflection on the powerful attraction of the East for European readers. Ricardo ensures himself a good audience for the triumphant scene of return by ostentatiously displaying the trappings of a good captivity tale: beautiful women in revealing Eastern garb and bloodthirsty, turbaned Turks.

Yet at a deeper level the excess of transvestism in the scene—perhaps clearest in the redundant disguise of Mahamut, who was surely dressed as a Turk already—seems profoundly odd. It suggests a strange reciprocity between Turks and Christians: if the former disguise themselves *a la cristianesca* to do their dastardly deeds, the latter dress morbidly *a la turquesca* without any readily apparent reason. Why the superfluous disguise, the desire to pass when returning in every way to one's true self—home, family, religion?[30] After all, a Turkish ship coming ashore on Sicily is hardly humorous, and Ricardo's an-

ticipated pleasure in anagnorisis contrasts strangely with Leonisa's shudders
as she remembers the distress she suffered along the selfsame coast (183). When
the townspeople spy the white turbans of those on board and worriedly prepare to defend themselves, the narrator tells us that the disguised Christians
"recibieron gran contento" (185) (were most pleased). This pleasure calls into
question their earlier protestations that they take to shameful dissimulation
strictly because their captivity demands it (170, 173); once free, they seem to
forget any notion of what they owe to being who they are for the sake of making a spectacular entrance. As Smith incisively notes, "Ricardo mimics the
turncoat, playfully reversing the vestimentary codes through which cultural
identities are produced and recognized."[31] The returning Christians bring back
to Sicily the excess and exoticism of Islam, from the decorated ship to Leonisa's
fabulous Moorish costume. In another, attenuated version of the auction scene,
Ricardo plays the role of Leonisa's master: still dressed in his turban, he makes
a present of her to the bewildered Cornelio, only to realize in midspeech that
she is not in fact his to give (186). Still dressed as a Turk, Ricardo finally becomes truly *liberal* as he realizes that his generosity cannot extend to giving
away what belongs to no one. His retraction somewhat counters his impersonation of a slaveholder, yet it cannot erase the powerful image of an entire
shipload of Christians capriciously passing as Turks.

The surfeit of passing is especially intriguing because the novella has already
taught us to be wary of the pleasures afforded by costume: it is Leonisa's en-
hanced beauty when dressed as a Moor that precipitates the violence and be-
trayals among the Turks. Moreover, the text suggests early on that a pleasurable appearance may in fact be indistinguishable from essence. As Ricardo
attacks Cornelio's manhood, at the beginning of his embedded narrative, he
taunts him with the story of Ulysses' rescue of the cross-dressed Achilles: "—Si
esa tu reposada condición tuviera Aquiles, bien seguro estuviera Ulises de no
salir con su empresa, aunque más le mostrara resplandecientes armas y acera-
dos alfanjes" (144–45) ("Had Achilles been as placid as you, Ulysses would certainly never have succeeded in his design, no matter how many shining arms
and sharp scimitars he might have shown him"). The story, related by Ulysses
himself in book 13 of the *Metamorphoses*, features the famous trickster unveil-
ing Achilles' essential masculinity. Thetis, foreseeing her son's fate, disguises
Achilles as a girl to save him from death in battle, but when Ulysses places weapons among the feminine frippery, Achilles promptly reaches for shield and lance.

In the counterscenario that Ricardo describes, Cornelio's feminine appearance—all "blandas manos y rizos cabellos, de voz meliflua y de amorosas palabras, y, finalmente, todo hecho de ámbar y de alfeñique, guarnecido de telas

y adornado de brocados" (143) (soft hands and curly locks, of honeyed voice and loving words, and, finally, all made of ambergris and almond paste, dressed in fine clothes and adorned with brocades)—matches his essence. No number of shiny weapons, not even the sharp scimitars that so suggestively foreshadow Ricardo's own eventual disguise, will bring out a manliness that is not there.[32] In fact, the entire romance tradition that Ricardo evokes in his tirade is turned on its head by the novella: unlike Ariosto's Ruggiero on Alcina's island or Tasso's Rinaldo on Armida's, the enervated warrior in this Sicilian bower ("—¿por qué no te levantas de ese estrado de flores?" [144] ["why don't you rise from that bed of flowers?"]) has not been enchanted or led astray by feminine wiles.[33] His is a permanently effeminate condition, unchanged by the end of the novella, that implicitly challenges the Western ascription of femininity and weakness to an Eastern threat. At this point, a number of interesting connections to "Las dos doncellas" become apparent: there, a young man named Adorno is persuaded by virile damsels that the Roman Mark Antony's trajectory is preferable to that of Aeneas; here in Sicily, the much-adorned Cornelio remains impervious to Ricardo's claims that there is anything wrong with his softness. In both cases the association of the East with indolence, disorder, and a noxious effeminacy is implicitly challenged.[34]

Cornelio—the only main character who does not spend time among the Turks—is both the most transparent and the least manly in the novella. Although he does not literally cross-dress, his feminine appearance troubles the ideological certainties of the text. The sodomitic threat of Islam—which looms so large in most Spanish accounts—remains largely unvoiced here.[35] Instead, it is refracted and internalized in a "new Ganymede," as Ricardo calls him (144), who has not been perverted by the Turks or forced in captivity but simply relishes what his own culture regards as effeminate. Cornelio's unforced effeminacy parallels Ricardo's unaccountable transvestism at the end: neither can be explained from within the rigid categories of Spanish ideology. Their respective affinities for feminine adornments and for Turkish costume are both carefully distinguished from each other and suggestively juxtaposed. Together, they undermine the masculinist Christian identity that Ricardo should, by rights, represent. The thematics of sartorial excess, which improbably connects the hero and his foil, counters the straitened cultural logic of the story: although Leonisa finally chooses the heroic and generous Ricardo over the effeminate Cornelio, her choice follows the reimportation of so-called Turkish mores—excess, exoticism, dissimulation—into Sicily by the hero himself. The pleasures of passing are, if anything, more closely associated with Christians than with Turks.

Violent Empires

The multiple scenes of cross-cultural transvestism in "El amante liberal" that I describe drive home the fluidity between Christianity and Islam in the eastern Mediterranean. More important, they proffer the bewildering interchangeability of the two as a key for reading the text. At a metatextual level, passing becomes a rhetorical strategy of dissimulation, enabling a sotto voce critique of Spain. Once the text has established that Turks and Christians are constantly dressing up as one another, it can cloak its pointed censure of Spanish ways in a highly orthodox critique of the Turk. The novella thus expands its ironic purview from the fragility of individual identities in a liminal space to the much heftier target of imperial practices within Spain and beyond. In what passes for a conventional denunciation of Turkish ways, the text mounts an often scathing critique of very Spanish habits.

Shortly after the story opens, and before Ricardo launches into the "confused labyrinth" of his troubles, he insists that Mahamut explain to him the transfer of power from one "virrey o bajá, como los turcos llaman a los virreyes" (140) (viceroy or pasha, as the Turks call viceroys) to the next. The narrative thus introduces us into the expected maze of adventures via a particularly roundabout path, one that leads away from Ricardo's story. Mahamut obliges, launching into a critique of the "violent empire" of the Turks. I quote at length to give some sense of the wealth of detail in the renegade's "brief" account:

> has de saber que es costumbre entre los turcos que los que van por virreyes de alguna provincia no entran en la ciudad donde su antecesor habita hasta que él salga della y deje hacer libremente al que viene la residencia; y en tanto que el bajá nuevo la hace, el antiguo se está en la campaña esperando lo que resulta de sus cargos, los cuales se le hacen sin que él pueda intervenir a valerse de sobornos ni amistades, si ya primero no lo ha hecho. Hecha, pues, la residencia, se la dan al que deja el cargo en un pergamino cerrado y sellado, y con ella se presenta a la Puerta del Gran Señor, que es como decir en la Corte ante un Gran Consejo del Turco; la cual vista por el visir-bajá, y por los otros cuatro bajáes menores, como si dijésemos ante el presidente del Real Consejo y oidores, o le premian o le castigan, según la relación de la residencia; puesto que si viene culpado, con dineros rescata y excusa el castigo. Si no viene culpado y no le premian, como sucede de ordinario, con dádivas y presentes alcanza el cargo que más se le antoja, porque no se dan allí los cargos y oficios por merecimientos, sino por dineros: todo se vende y todo se compra. Los proveedores de los cargos roban [a] los proveídos en ellos y los desuellan; deste oficio comprado sale la sustancia para comprar otro que más ganancia promete. Todo va como digo, todo este imperio es violento, señal que prometía no ser durable; pero a lo que yo creo, y así debe de ser verdad, le tienen sobre

sus hombros nuestro pecados, quiero decir, los de aquellos que descaradamente y a rienda suelta ofenden a Dios, como yo hago. (140–41)

[You should know that it is customary among the Turks for those who are sent as viceroys to a province not to enter the city where their predecessor lives until he leaves it and allows the one who arrives to carry out his inspection; and while the new pasha conducts it, the old one waits in the countryside for whatever charges may result, which are brought against him without his being able to intervene to avail himself of bribery or friendship, if he has not done so already. Once the report is completed, it is handed in a closed and sealed parchment to the outgoing viceroy, who presents himself with it at the Porte of the Great Lord, which is as if to say in the court before a Great Council of the Turk; and once it is examined by the vizier-pasha and by the other four minor pashas, or, as we might say, before the president of the Royal Council and the judges, they either reward or punish him, according to the narrative of the report, although if he is deemed guilty he can redeem himself and avoid the punishment with money. If he is not deemed guilty and they do not reward him, as generally occurs, with gifts and favors, then he acquires the post that he most desires, because posts and offices are not given there for merit but for money: everything is bought and everything is sold. The bestowers of positions steal from those on whom they are bestowed and fleece them; from one office bought comes the wherewithal for buying another that promises greater profit. It all happens as I say, the whole empire is violent, a sign that it promises not to last; but I believe, and it must be true, that our sins support it on their shoulders, that is, the sins of those who offend God brazenly and without restraint, as I do.]

Why this incredibly detailed exposé of Turkish institutions, with a mea culpa for the surprising endurance of the corrupt and violent empire at the end? At one level, Mahamut's speech rehearses the commonplace Orientalist attributions of corruption and intrigue to the Turks, while acknowledging the crucial role of renegades within the Ottoman Empire.[36] Whether or not his detailed description corresponds to Turkish practices, however, it recalls in no uncertain terms the processes, documents, and offices of the Spanish imperial bureaucracy. From the initial translation provided by Ricardo ("como los turcos llaman a los *virreyes*") to the account of *residencias, relaciones,* and *consejos,* the description of Turkish ways sounds uncannily Spanish.[37] The linguistic equivalence, as Spanish terms stand in for Turkish ones, establishes the link between the two polities.[38] More important, it signals a more expansive rhetorical maneuver by which a critique of the Spanish Empire can, in effect, pass as a critique of the Turks.[39]

Mahamut's tone wavers between admiration for practices meant to avoid corruption ("sin que él pueda intervenir a valerse de sobornos y amistades") and a cynical conviction that the safeguards are in vain ("si ya primero no lo ha hecho"). There is a devastating irony in the throwaway "como sucede de ordinario" to describe the lack of compensation for worthy officials. Grammatical ambiguity compounds the sarcasm: "con dádivas y presentes" does not modify the "premian" that precedes it, as might at first appear, but instead the "alcanza el cargo" that follows. Thus the very structure of the phrase enacts the confusion that ensues when bribes stand in for rewards. Mahamut's condemnation mounts until he summarily concludes, "Todo este imperio es violento." Yet it is important to recall that he began on a note of approval for the attempted transparency of the Turkish *residencia*.[40] The combination of praise and censure makes his speech particularly slippery, since it multiplies the possibilities for identification and contrast. The Turkish Empire is both like and unlike Spain—similar enough that the criticism voiced by the renegade strikes home; dissimilar enough to function as a counterexample of a (dis)ordered polity.[41]

More transparent moments of praise for the Turks underscore the contrast between Turkish and Spanish bureaucracies. The narrator himself provides a wealth of detail on the judicial proceedings that accompany the viceroyal transfer of power, noting that they are open to Christian Greeks as well as to Turks. He stresses the simplicity of the proceedings, as befits simple cases:

> las más despachó el Cadí sin dar traslado a la parte, sin autos, demandas ni respuestas, que todas las causas, si no son las matrimoniales, se despachan en pie y en un punto, más a juicio de buen varón que por ley alguna. Y entre aquellos bárbaros, si lo son en esto, el cadí es el juez competente de todas las causas, que las abrevia en la uña y las sentencia en un soplo, sin que haya apelación de su sentencia para otro tribunal. (156)

> [the *cadí* settled most of them without referring them, without edicts, suits, or formal statements, for all cases, except those relating to marriage, are decided immediately, more according to a good man's judgment than to any law. And among those barbarians, if they are so in this respect, the *cadí* is the judge in all cases, fitting them in a nutshell and sentencing them in a flash, with no possibility of his sentence being appealed in another tribunal.]

"Si lo son en esto." The passage challenges the stereotype of a barbaric, despotic empire by suggesting that the concentration of power in one good man paradoxically minimizes the abuse of power, preventing delays and repeated opportunities for corruption. The simple resolution of petty cases contrasts most markedly with the depravity of the Turkish officials as they wrestle for Leonisa, disguising their lust as the fitting acquisition of presents for the Great Lord. Yet it also contrasts implicitly with the inefficiencies of Spain's complex legal system, plagued by delays and venality.[42] Clearly, the text does not set up the Ottoman Empire as an uncomplicated model for Spain to follow; instead, it marks the positive differences in the expediency of Ottoman justice while underscoring the similarities in corruption.

Perhaps the most powerful criticism of Spain in "El amante liberal" depends on its juxtaposition with another novella. Cervantes's prologue, it must be remembered, recommends reading the tales for the "sabroso y honesto fruto que se podría sacar, así de todas juntas, como de cada una por sí" (52) (tasty and honest fruit that one might gather from all of them together, as from each individual one). If one takes seriously the ordering of Cervantes's collection, the intertextual ironies become patent: "La gitanilla," which immediately precedes "El amante liberal" and is set entirely in Spain, candidly shows both gypsies and nobles greasing the palms of the authorities and subverting justice with gold.[43] Preciosa, the noble gypsy, suggests to one official that he take bribes in order to pay for his entertainment. She has heard "que de los oficios se ha de sacar dineros para pagar las condenaciones de las residencias y para pretender otros cargos" (81) (that from a post you must make money with which to pay the penalties from the inspection and solicit other positions). Or, as Mahamut might put it, "todo se vende y todo se compra."[44] Juan de Cárcamo, Preciosa's noble wooer, attempts to impress her with his father's suit at court for a position; by the end of the novella we learn that he has been appointed *corregidor* and will succeed Preciosa's newly discovered and manifestly corrupt father in that office. (What the latter's *residencia* might have yielded, we are never told. But if the novella itself is read as a mock *relación* of the events, it provides more than sufficient evidence to condemn him.) The first novella thus ends with a Spanish change of authorities that anticipates the change of Turkish viceroys at the beginning of the second. "La gitanilla"'s more explicit critique of venality at the heart of Spain necessarily informs any reading of Turkish corruption in the novella that follows. The juxtaposition nudges the reader to recognize the similarities between worlds that may seem very different. Thus the intertextuality compounds the ironic effect of the *intra*textual passing, as "La gitanilla" literally brings home the exotic matter of "El amante liberal" and its imperial critique in Turkish guise.

"El amante liberal" imagines the eastern Mediterranean as a space both fluid and chaotic, where, despite the religious divide, competing empires overlap both geographically and conceptually. To ground the exotic vision of Oriental confusion, the novella constantly invokes Spain—from its colonial stand-in (Sicily), to the imperial exploits of Charles V, to its bureaucratic institutions. The allusions complicate the relation between colonial space and metropolis: in some cases, as with the easy repatriation of renegades, the former implicitly indicts the latter. In this sense, the easy resolution of the narrative functions as the most scathing critique of an intolerant Spain: despite the ambiguity of

Mahamut, the flimsy motivations of Halima, Leonisa's Moorish garb, and Ricardo's penchant for playing Turk, Sicily remains open and available to them. The only unresolved issue at the end—the unmatched and weeping Cornelio—upends traditional stereotypes of Eastern effeminacy, locating the ostensible threat to Western masculinity squarely within Spanish territory. Both religious and gender ambiguity are thus firmly planted behind Spanish lines as the passing pleasures of a Byzantine fantasy harden into a critique of a muscularly Christian Spain.

Performing Inclusion

La gran sultana Doña Catalina de Oviedo enacts an oxymoronic mixture of Turk and Christian in its very title—it is an Eastern tale with an Asturian Old Christian protagonist. At a number of levels the *comedia* resolves the contradictions that feature so prominently in "El amante liberal" by making hybridity into a permanent condition. Thus the temporary passing between Christianity and Islam in the novella is here taken much farther than simple disguise into a more profound sense of personal transformation with the promise of actual *mestizaje* in future generations.[45] Much as in "El amante liberal," however, the treatment of passing itself relativizes the ideological certainties of masculinist Christian ideology to suggest instead the powerful appeal of a permeable Ottoman world.

This "*mirage turc,*" as Jean Canavaggio dubs it, has generally been read as a Byzantine fantasy.[46] However, like the so-called idealist novellas that I discuss, the play has a fascinating historical dimension. It tells the story of the young Spanish captive Catalina, who grows into a great beauty in the seraglio while hidden by a sympathetic renegade. When she is finally presented to Sultan Amurates, he falls so completely in love with her that he decides to marry her, allowing her to remain a Christian and generally acceding to her requests. Under pressure from his advisors, who urge him to produce an heir, he is forced to turn to others in his seraglio, but Catalina triumphantly wins him back when she announces that she is already pregnant with his child—a future "otomano español" (Spanish Ottoman).[47] While the plot rehearses familiar tropes from the Byzantine romances and the Italian novella tradition, it is also full of historically accurate details. As Albert Mas and Canavaggio both show, "Amurates" corresponds quite closely to Venetian ambassadors' account of Sultan Murad III (d. 1595) and his love for the Corfiote Christian captive Safidje.[48] Thus Cervantes does not invent the figure of a sultana who favors Christians— she is already well established in the historical sources; rather, his primary departure is the complete fabrication of her Spanish identity.

Clearly the change makes Catalina a more gripping character where Spanish audiences were concerned. Her "desenfado español" (390) (Spanish verve) is, her pander Mamí tells Amurates, the crowning touch on her beauty. Yet, although she steadfastly adheres to Christianity and exercises great power over the sultan, Catalina hardly represents a militant, unyielding Spain.[49] In fact, her success in the Ottoman court stems primarily from her strategic recognition of her own limits and her flexibility in adapting to her situation—a marked contrast to the Christian martyrs of Cervantes's North African *comedias*, *Los tratos de Argel* and *Los baños de Argel*. In the world of *La gran sultana*, Christian identity need not be preserved at the cost of one's life, largely because the Muslims are only too happy to allow the practice of Christianity. This representation corresponds much more closely to the reality of relative tolerance in the Muslim world than the vision of persecution so characteristic of the Algerian plays.[50]

Catalina's initial reaction to the sultan's desire is to dwell on the enormity of marrying a Muslim: "—¿No es grandísimo pecado / el juntarme a un infiel?" (ll. 1110–11) ("Is it not a huge sin to pair myself with an infidel?"). As the sympathetic renegade Rustán points out, however, the sultan is not forcing her to become a Muslim, and her desire for martyrdom is therefore misplaced:

Sultana: Mártir seré si consiento;
   antes morir que pecar.
Rustan: Ser mártir se ha de causar
   por más alto fundamento que es por el perder la vida
   por confesión de la fe.
Sultana: Esa ocasión tomaré.
Rustan: ¿Quién a ella te convida?
   Sultán te quiere cristiana . . . (ll. 1130–38)

[Sultana: I will be a martyr if I choose to die rather than to sin.
Rustan: Martyrdom stems from more weighty causes, namely, losing one's life
   because of confessing one's faith.
Sultana: I will take the opportunity to do that.
Rustan: Who is offering it to you? The sultan wants you as a Christian.]

Despite her initial penchant for martyrdom, Catalina gradually realizes how much religious freedom she may exercise as the sultan's consort. Not only is the Ottoman ruler unwilling to force himself upon her, but he is only too glad to accommodate her Christian faith and remains strikingly open-minded where her religious practices are concerned:

¿Tengo yo a cargo tu alma,
o soy Dios para inclinalla,

o ya de hecho llevalla
donde alcance eterna palma?
Vive tú a tu parecer,
como no vivas sin mí. (ll. 1242–47)

[Am I responsible for your soul, or am I God to influence it or even lead it to eternal glory? Live as you see fit, as long as you do not live without me.]

The sultan's matter-of-fact forbearance occasionally shades into a more servile admiration of Spanish valor; in general, however, he magnanimously grants Catalina's wishes without diminishing his own power. She insists on keeping her own name and on dressing as a Spaniard, but, despite a complex subplot that brings her father to the court disguised as a Christian tailor, her attire does not change the basic fact of her fecund union with the sultan and of her permanent place in the Muslim world. While not a renegade, she has crossed over in crucial ways. She exists as a Christian at the heart of the Ottoman Empire, yet, despite the sultan's promises, her power is largely limited to controlling her own person and occasionally seeking mercy for Christians. When her father accusingly observes that she shows no physical traces of force and therefore must have yielded willingly to the sultan, Catalina grants that she yielded "por quedarme / con el nombre de cristiana" (ll. 2005–6) (in order to keep my Christian name). Thus, while she remains an admirable character, her achievement is due not so much to her own intransigence as to the Turks' ability to incorporate difference and transform it into a source of strength. As the sultan puts it, with his tolerance,

no hago ningún extremo,
si ya no fuese el de hacer
que con la sangre otomana
mezcle la tuya cristiana
para darle mayor ser. (ll. 1205–9)

[I do nothing extreme, except perhaps to mix Ottoman blood with your Christian blood to make it greater.]

The mixture itself is presented as a source of strength. The sultan's perspective, George Mariscal notes, "strikes at the very heart of ideologies of purity. In a single stroke it problematizes rigid categories of religion, nation, and ethnicity and proposes a by no means undesirable (in the logic of this particular *comedia*) cultural and genetic synthesis."[51] Although the mestizo generation is never actually staged, the *comedia* provides abundant evidence of Ottoman increase in a subplot of gender and religious passing that underscores the appeal of Turkish tolerance.

The play's most interesting exchanges occur among the supporting characters in the harem, where the Transylvanian captive Lamberto hides, disguised as the beautiful maiden Zelinda. After eloping with his beloved Clara and being captured by Turks, Lamberto cross-dresses to follow his bride into the harem but remains masculine enough to impregnate her, even in such dire straits. When the sultan reluctantly agrees to stray from his beloved Catalina for the sake of siring plentiful heirs, he fatefully chooses Lamberto among all the women in the seraglio. As Ellen Anderson points out, the sultan's uneager choice functions as a "playful parody of the demonic homosexual pedophilia of the Algerian plays."[52] Alternatively, it underscores how successfully the Christian Lamberto, effeminized by his love for Clara, passes as a woman. When the sultan, outraged, discovers him to be a man, Lamberto quickly makes up a story of transsexual change to explain his embarrassing masculinity.

Marvelous narratives of sexual transformation from woman to man had a certain currency in the late sixteenth century: to some extent they were held to confirm the Galenic tradition that regarded female genitalia as imperfect, undescended mirror images of male organs. In exceptional circumstances the "natural" progress of the sex organs toward their perfected state could invert a woman's sex, rendering her male. Both Montaigne and the surgeon Ambroise Paré, for example, record the story of a peasant girl named Marie whose male organs descended when she bounded over a ditch in the fields, suddenly transforming her/him into "Germain."[53] But Lamberto's fabrication gives the transformation a particular religious slant, tying it to his liminal position as a Christian captive at the heart of Islam. Years of pleading with Heaven for masculinity as a Christian were to no avail, he claims, but conversion to Islam brought the desired change:

> Lamberto: Siendo niña, a un varón sabio
> oí decir las excelencias
> y mejoras que tenía
> el hombre más que la hembra;
> desde allí me aficioné
> a ser varón, de manera
> que le pedí esta merced
> al Cielo con asistencia.
> Cristiana me la negó,
> y mora no me la niega.
> Mahoma, a quien hoy gimiendo,
> con lágrimas y terneza,
> con fervorosos deseos,
> con votos y con promesas,

con ruegos y con suspiros
que a una roca enternecieran,
desde el serrallo hasta aquí,
en silencio y con inmensa
eficacia, le he pedido
me hiciese merced tan nueva.
Acudió a mis ruegos tiernos,
enternecido, el Profeta,
y en un instante volvióme
en fuerte varón de hembra;
y si por tales milagros
se merece alguna pena,
vuelva el Profeta por mí,
y por mi inocencia vuelva. (ll. 2721–48)

[As a girl I heard a wise man describe the excellence and advantages that man has over woman; from that point on I wanted to be male, so I asked Heaven for this mercy with its help. As a Christian woman it was denied to me, but not as a Moorish woman. I have begged Mohammed to grant me this novel mercy, moaning with tears and endearments, with fervent desires, with vows and promises, with prayers and sighs that would move a rock, all the way from the seraglio, silently and with great efficacy. Touched, the Prophet responded to my tender prayers and in an instant turned me from a woman into a strong man, and if such miracles deserve punishment, let the Prophet return for me and for my innocence.]

Lamberto's narrative proclaims not one but two crucial transformations, as gender transvestism collapses into a hasty religious conversion. Before he can explain his masculinity, he must convert himself into a *mora*. Although he stages the double transformation to fool a menacing audience, the religious conversion, like his originary masculinity, *sticks*. That is, although the story of sexual transformation is a complete fabrication—"Zelinda" has been a male all along—the religious transformation that s/he concocts takes on a reality of its own. The joke is ostensibly on the credulous sultan, who believes Lamberto's miraculous fable, yet an actual transformation has in fact been effected. The captive who, with his lover, had recently protested their desire to die "cristianos en todo caso" (l. 1459) (Christians by all means) effectively rejects his faith and embraces Islam. In a more desperate situation than Catalina, he chooses accommodation over martyrdom.

Beyond the humor of the cross-dressing and the false sex-change lies a striking departure from the more traditional European literary depictions of Islam. The tradition emphasizes conversions to Christianity and renegades—

like Mahamut in "El amante liberal"—who return *from* Islam to rejoin the Christian fold. Lamberto's story and its reception thus mark more than the sultan's credulity. They point also to the comparative advantage afforded Islam by its relative openness to renegades and its unwillingness to delve too deeply into the authenticity of conversion as long as its forms are observed. Lamberto's fate underscores the political expedience of this approach. The Christian sultana, Catalina, intercedes in favor of the captive lovers, requesting that Lamberto be appointed pasha of Chios. The sultan not only grants the favor but augments it, naming him instead governor of Rhodes—a much more significant and sensitive appointment. The implicit understanding is that, regardless of his religious authenticity, his political allegiance has in fact transferred over to Islam insofar as is necessary for him to hold such a position. Thus, the fantastic story of sexual transformation becomes instead an allegory for the openness of an empire that refuses to ask too many questions of those it employs, benefiting instead from even the most improbable acts of allegiance.

Lamberto's transvestism marks a set of complicated transactions between masculinity and religious allegiance: the Christian captive manages to salvage his masculinity after effeminization in the seraglio, yet he himself characterizes that masculinity as a product of his apostasy and defection to Islam. Moreover, once he is appointed governor of Rhodes, his conversion acquires a political as well as a personal dimension. The cross-dressed captive's passing becomes a permanent transformation, not of gender, but of religious and political affiliation. While Mohammed does not grant Lamberto his masculinity, the episode obliquely acknowledges Islam's acceptance of renegades as a source of Ottoman military strength.

Strikingly, none of the Christian characters I discuss return to Christendom; at the end of the *comedia* Catalina, Lamberto, and Clara all seem firmly ensconced within the Ottoman world. The only one to return to Spain is Madrigal, the *gracioso* who voices nationalist and anti-Semitic prejudice but has himself passed up earlier opportunities for repatriation because of his involvement with a Muslim woman. Nowhere does *La gran sultana* evince the teleological emphasis on freedom that is so prevalent in other stories of captivity. Instead, it imagines an Ottoman world of such permeability and fluidity that Christian captives with varying degrees of commitment to their faith can rise to prominence and power. Unlike "El amante liberal," which concludes with a return to Christendom, however problematic, *La gran sultana* stages lasting accommodations and transformations that never lead back to Europe. The pleasure of passing, so vividly described in the novella, here builds into a more permanent allegiance to a welcoming empire. At a time when Spain had decreed the permanent expulsion of all Moriscos and was increasingly closing its doors to all converts, however sincere, the vision of an aggressively inclusive Ottoman world reads as an oblique reproach and a potent reminder of the political and military costs of religious authenticity and enforced transparency.

5

"La disimulación es provechosa": The Critique of Transparency in the *Persiles* and "La española inglesa"

> Seguí las costumbres de mi patria, a lo menos en cuanto a las que
> parecían ser niveladas con la razón, y en las que no, con apariencias
> fingidas mostraba seguirlas, que tal vez la disimulación es provechosa.
>
> [I followed the customs of my country, at least insofar as they
> seemed to be reasonable, while I gave the appearance of following
> those that didn't, for sometimes pretense is to one's advantage.]
>
> —Mauricio, in Cervantes's *Los trabajos de Persiles y Sigismunda*

First-time readers of *Los trabajos de Persiles y Sigismunda* (The trials of Persiles and Sigismunda) might well wonder where on earth the title characters are. This is not a question of identifying the bewildering landscapes traversed by "Periandro," "Auristela," and their companions—generations of critics have carefully mapped the exotic northern lands of books I and II and the European trajectories of books III and IV. Instead, it is the far more basic issue of locating title characters who are not even mentioned until the middle of the text or revealed until the very end, in chapter 12 of book IV, "donde se dice quién era Periandro y Auristela" (464) ("where we learn who Periandro and Auristela were" [341]). The fantastically prolonged disguise of the protagonists makes of the *Persiles* a kind of transvestite text in which the ostensible subject matter is constantly disguised, as are the actual subjects of the narrative.[1] The dynamics of passing that I analyze earlier here become a veritable narrative principle as the sustained impersonations challenge the reader's attempt to pin down the elusive protagonists and render them fully legible. Yet, as I argue in this chapter, their opacity is precisely the point—an oblique but powerful counter to any discriminatory impulse. Thus, these central characters bear a striking resemblance to such apparently marginal figures as Ana Félix in part II of *Don Quijote* and the multiply passing Lamberto in *La gran sultana:* they elude classification, thereby problematizing the very categories that organize Spanish orthodoxy.

It is difficult to shake the impression that the passing characters actually *are* Periandro and Auristela, since they are called by those names until the last minute. Paradoxically, their "true" identities as Persiles and Sigismunda seem artificial, while their assumed identities connote all their adventures and pronouncements throughout the text. Critics have silently acknowledged this strange feature of the *Persiles,* almost universally referring to the protagonists by their assumed names. They are, we imply, who they say they are for hundreds of pages. Sheer perseverance in disguise affords them aliases far more authentic that any "real" identity.

Cervantes's conceit of disguising his main characters complicates the literary conventions of anagnorisis. The text begins darkly, in medias res; we are only gradually introduced to the protagonists and informed of their (assumed) names. Unlike in "Las dos doncellas," however, the identities initially revealed here are not authentic but a conscious fabrication: we are still at least one layer away from the truth. Auristela may, like the damsels, resort to cross-dressing, but when the male attire is peeled away, her identity is still disguised. The more profound revelations at the end are also unusual in that they disclose nothing to the protagonists themselves. Whereas Preciosa of "La gitanilla" or Perdita of Shakespeare's *A Winter's Tale* are as surprised as anyone to discover who they really are, Auristela and Periandro knew all along. Theirs is a deliberate dissimulation consciously undertaken—a very different matter from the romance motif of the stolen or lost infant miraculously restored.

Far from tantalizing the reader with the mystery, the text emphatically condemns the urge to know. Discovering the characters' identity, piercing their disguise—these are immoral and dangerous pursuits here. The *Persiles* functions as a kind of antidetective novel: despite the implicit promise of a revelation in the obscure title, the point is to disarm readerly curiosity as the narrative meanders along fascinating byways. In this chapter I argue that the transvestite *Persiles* mounts a sustained critique of the inquisitorial investigation of lineage and blood in Counter-Reformation Spain by suggesting that assumed and deracinated selves are as valid as "authentic," well-documented ones.[2] Similar to "La española inglesa," the *Persiles* valorizes dissimulation and discreet oversight while explicitly condemning close scrutiny. The broad textual wink that advocates deliberate oversight—*hacer la vista gorda*—functions as a critique of the discriminatory and repressive practices associated with the enforced revelation of subjects' identities and the inquisitorial eye.

Reading for the Plot

To summarize the plot of the *Persiles* necessarily involves upending the delicate mechanisms of dissimulation and revelation that I describe above. In brief, the novel traces the adventures of a pair of noble and chaste lovers, Persiles and Sigismunda, who pass as the siblings Periandro and Auristela while they travel, largely via shipwreck, from the far confines of the world—the brutal Barbarian Isle on which the narrative opens—to Rome. Their centripetal journey is neatly divided into exotic northern travels and a more familiar European pilgrimage through Portugal, Spain, France, and Italy. They acquire a number of sporadic companions, of whom the most constant are Arnaldo, the prince of Denmark and indefatigable suitor to Auristela, and the "mestizo" family of Antonio, a Spaniard who was shipwrecked on the Barbarian Isle, his wife, Ricla, and their children, Antonio and Constanza.[3] While book II includes an extensive retrospective narration by Periandro that serves to clarify previous events, books I and III often neglect the protagonists in favor of the interpolated adventures of other unfortunate lovers. Even Periandro's narration, as I discuss below, includes a number of disparate stories. These episodes, only loosely connected by the voyage of the protagonists, make up the bulk of the *Persiles*. The central plot remains so obscure as to appear largely incidental: only at the end is it revealed that Persiles and Sigismunda were sent to Rome by his mother on the pretext of strengthening Sigismunda's faith but in actuality so that she might marry Persiles and not his elder brother, Magsimino, for whom she was intended.

Given the constant movement toward Rome, critics such as Alban Forcione have attempted to order the *Persiles*'s multiplicity by reading it as an allegory of Christian fall and redemption.[4] Clearly, the attainment of Christian virtue is a central theme of the text. Yet the quest reading, though powerful, imposes the same teleological—even anagogic—bias that characterizes the central Christian narrative. Moreover, as Antonio Márquez points out, it overlooks the text's own ambivalence about Auristela's motivations for traveling to Rome.[5] While she does seek out Christian doctrine upon her arrival and experiences spiritual fulfillment in the city, the ostensible vow that she must satisfy is repeatedly presented as an excuse for escaping unwanted suitors.[6] A retrospective reading suggests that Auristela's quest was above all a pretext for escape.

Forcione also argues that "nearly all the episodes of the *Persiles* repeat the cyclical rhythm of the main plot."[7] While the interpolated narrations are thematically linked and often illustrate the main plot, they can hardly be sub-sumed into one category or reduced to minor versions of the protagonists' odyssey.[8] Instead, they seem designed precisely to counter the teleological thrust of the voyage to Rome. If, as Márquez suggests in discussing the *Persiles,* "La forma es el contenido ideológico de la obra de ficción" (form is the ideological content of a work of fiction),[9] then this text seems committed to delay and digression. The dilation of the plot becomes most pronounced in book III, which includes six separate interpolated stories of love and revenge in which, with one exception, the protagonists play relatively small roles. The geographical progress across Europe to Rome is interrupted by narrative detours that detract from the suspense of the main plot until the reader is no longer fixated on the revelation of Periandro's and Auristela's identities. Even the characters seem more individualized, and certainly more compelling, in the interpolated stories than in the main narrative: who would not rather read about Ambrosia Agustina, the transvestite damsel who follows her new husband to war in order to consummate their union, or about Isabela Castrucha, who feigns demonic possession in order to marry the man she loves, than about the matchless Auristela? This seems precisely the point: the narrative diversions effectively neutralize the suspense of the main plot. The technique is markedly not one of interlacing—the romance style that interweaves multiple story lines—but a more blatant and repeated postponement of the main plot.[10] The digressions seem so successful in this regard that at one point the narrator must transparently haul readers back to Periandro and Auristela with the dramatic story of the *mujer voladora,* the "flying woman" of book III, chapter 14. The pilgrims encounter a woman atop a tall tower desperately crying for help; Periandro rushes to save her from her crazed husband and suffers a near mortal fall, while the woman's voluminous skirts allow her to float gently to the ground. In despair, Auristela lets drop some intriguing hints as to Periandro's origins: "—¡Cuán cierta la tendrá la reina, vuestra madre, cuando a sus oídos llegue vuestra no pensada muerte!" (376) ("'The queen, your mother, will be certain to die when she learns of your unexpected death!'" [271]), which, we are pointedly told, intrigue the bystanders. But this tantalizing interlude is the exception rather than the rule: in general, the supposed protagonists fade into the frame of the interpolated tales.

The *Persiles* constantly thematizes its own preoccupation with dilation and revelation, identity and disguise. Critics often comment on Periandro's drawn-out narrative of his adventures in book II and the largely negative responses of his audience.[11] While Auristela and their friends anxiously await their departure from the dangerous court of King Policarpo, Periandro leisurely and self-consciously recounts his travails. Much like the main narrative, his begins in medias res, aboard a pirate ship. While it provides great detail on the wedding customs of fisherpeople, their boat races, and the marital troubles of northern kings, it leaves us in the dark as to Periandro's origins. Thus, this second partial narrative, offered as a means of clarifying the primary one, actually clarifies very little.

Given the similarities between the main narrative and Periandro's embedded yarn, the reader's impatience with the latter functions also as a critique of the *Persiles* itself. The astrologer Mauricio, the most vocal and persistent critic of Periandro's narration, focuses on the Aristotelian problem of unity: "los episodios que por ornato de las historias se ponen no han de ser tan grandes como la misma historia" (234) ("episodes included to adorn the story shouldn't be as long as the story itself" [159]). And Periandro does show a real penchant for episodic adornment. More important, however, his narrative in toto looms large within the *Persiles* without adding to the forward movement of the plot or clarifying the protagonists' stories. Why draw attention to Periandro's digression and implicitly criticize the *Persiles* itself? As Américo Castro first suggested, and Stanislav Zimic underscores, Cervantes wants it both ways: he relishes the narrative possibilities of digressive romance even as he frames the genre's foibles with critical metacommentary.[12] While Castro's insight clarifies the formal dynamics here, it tells us little about the ideological importance of digression. The repeated criticisms of Periandro's excursus function, I argue, as hermeneutic signposts, reminding us that there is a fundamental tension between reading for the end and focusing on messy middles. Mauricio's impatient response is not unanimous—the female audience is generally more sympathetic—and even he admits that Periandro's narration is pleasurable. The protracted yarn and its explicit critique within the text thus stress the many possible modes of reading: one could approach the *Persiles* as Mauricio does Periandro's tale—that is, in a relentless search for unity and resolution—or opt instead for a less teleological mode and relish the digressions.

The Dangers of Discovery

The second mode, with less emphasis placed on the revelations at the end, is implicitly valorized by the text's condemnation of knowing readers who get ahead of themselves. If, as Mary Gaylord suggests, "the most challenging interpretive task, indeed the central assignment of the book, is that of 'reading' Auristela and Periandro,"[13] then it is surely odd how ruthlessly the text deals with the figure who most accurately sees through their dissimulation. The *maldiciente* Clodio, exiled from England for his satiric pronouncements, joins the protagonists on their northern voyages. From the moment he introduces himself there is no question that his skeptical inquisitiveness is highly noxious: "—Tengo un cierto espíritu satírico y maldiciente, una pluma veloz y una lengua libre; deléitanme las maliciosas agudezas, y por decir una, perderé yo, no sólo un amigo, pero cien mil vidas" (118) ("'I have a certain [satiric and slanderous spirit], a quick pen and a loose tongue; malicious quips delight me and to express just one I'd risk losing not only one friend but a hundred thousand lives'" [68]). Rosamunda, former mistress of the king of England, has been chained to Clodio in exile, her sexual freedom equated with the scandal of his tongue. She expands upon the insidious effects of his spirit in peculiarly Spanish terms: "—Tú has lastimado mil ajenas honras, has aniquilado ilustres créditos, has descubierto secretos escondidos y contaminado linajes claros" (119) ("'You've injured a thousand honors that didn't concern you, you've destroyed illustrious reputations, you've uncovered hidden secrets and contaminated pure lineages'" [68]).

Honra and *linaje* seem particularly vulnerable to Clodio's investigations, in a formulation that suggests the vulnerability of Spanish subjects in particular to accusations of "tainted blood." As Albert Sicroff points out, "given that genealogical investigations admitted such flimsy evidence as secret accusations and obscure rumors, how could one doubt that a man with bad intentions would be able to find two witnesses who would testify orally against a rival's purity of blood?"[14] Clodio argues that he has never actually slandered anyone, yet Rosamunda and Mauricio both make clear that even the truth does not justify his zeal:

> —Con todo eso—dijo Clodio—, jamás me ha acusado la conciencia de haber dicho alguna mentira.
> —A tener tú conciencia—dijo Rosamunda—de las verdades que has dicho tenías harto de que acusarte, que no todas las verdades han de salir en público, ni a los ojos de todos.
> —Sí—dijo a esta sazón Mauricio—, sí, que tiene razón Rosamunda, que las verdades de las culpas cometidas en secreto, nadie ha de ser osado de sacarlas en público. (119)

> "In spite of all you've said," spoke Clodio, "my conscience has never accused me of having told a single lie."
> "If you had a conscience," replied Rosamunda, "you'd have plenty to accuse yourself of, considering the truths you've told, for not every truth should be revealed in public for all eyes to see."
> "Yes," said Mauricio at this point, "yes, Rosamunda's right, for no one should dare bring out publicly the truth of wrongs committed in secret." (69)

The truth, these two suggest, is not necessarily beneficial, nor does it always belong in the public sphere. In the context of Counter-Reformation Spain, these blatant calls for dissimulation and discretion are quite remarkable. Rosamunda and Mauricio here argue clearly against revealing secret faults or blemishes in a subject's lineage—precisely the kinds of investigations required by the "clean blood" statutes. Their rejection of Clodio's inquisitorial zeal implicitly challenges the entire repressive apparatus sustained by those investigations. How could anyone discriminate against *conversos* if the taints in their lineage were to remain secret?

Swiftly established as the importunate revealer of hidden truths, Clodio turns to the enigma at hand. He first voices his skepticism about the true relationship between Periandro and Auristela to her spurned suitor, Prince Arnaldo:

> —has de considerar que algún gran misterio encierra desechar una mujer un reino y un príncipe que merece ser amado. Misterio también encierra ver una doncella vagabunda, llena de recato de encubrir su linaje, acompañada de un mozo que, como dice que lo es, podría no ser su hermano. (168)

> "you need to consider that there must be some great mystery involved when a woman rejects a kingdom and a prince worthy of her love. There is also something mysterious [in a vagabond damsel], cautiously concealing her lineage and accompanied by a young man who, although she says he's her brother, may not in fact be so." (107)

He insists on the problem of Auristela's origin, explicitly warning Arnaldo against marriage to a woman of unknown lineage:

> —Mira que los reyes están obligados a casarse, no con la hermosura, sino con el linaje; no con la riqueza, sino con la virtud, por la obligación que tienen de dar buenos sucesores a sus reinos. Desmengua y apoca el respeto que se debe al príncipe el verle cojear en la sangre, y no basta decir que la grandeza del rey es en sí tan poderosa que iguala consigo misma la bajeza de la mujer que escogiere. El caballo y la yegua de casta generosa y conocida, prometen crías de valor admirable, más que las no conocidas y de baja estirpe. (175)

> "Remember that kings have an obligation to marry not for beauty but for blood, not for riches but for virtue—out of the obligation they have to give their kingdoms good successors to follow them. The respect one should feel for a prince diminishes and decreases [when his blood is lacking], and it's not enough just to say a king's greatness can by itself make any woman he might choose his equal. The horse and mare of distinguished and illustrious breeding promise offspring of exceptional worth, much more so than those with an unknown and lowly pedigree." (113)

Clodio's initial concern with the mystery of Auristela's origins becomes an explicit fixation on genealogy and blood. His skeptical reading of Auristela goes against the traditions of romance that equate shining beauty and exceptional virtue with noble origins, however obscured. For Clodio, if the protagonists hide their origins it is because they have something to hide.

Clodio, whose concern goes beyond protecting the prince, shares his doubts with the former dancing master, Rutilio, in more general terms:

> —¿Qué diremos desta Auristela y deste su hermano, mozos vagabundos, encu-bridores de su linaje, quizá por poner en duda si son o no principales? Que el que está ausente de su patria, donde nadie le conoce, bien puede darse los pa-dres que quisiere, y con la discreción y artificio, parecer en sus costumbres que son hijos del sol y de la luna. (182)

> "What can we say about this Auristela and this brother of hers, young vagabonds who conceal their lineage, perhaps to cloud the question of whether or not they're highborn people? Anyone away from his homeland where no one knows him can easily give himself any parents he wishes, and with [discretion and artifice can appear by his behavior to be the child] of the sun and the moon." (119)

The voyage itself, Clodio reminds us, provides a perfect opportunity for passing as identities become untethered from their original contexts.[15]

As Castro points out, detaching oneself from one's habitual ties was a crucial precondition for successful passing as an Old Christian. He cites satirical recipes for constructing exemplary Spanish identities that obliquely confirm Clodio's point. In the early dramatist Lope de Rueda's *Comedia Medora*, the upwardly mobile son of an apothecary plans his transformation: "'"Lo prim-ero que haré será hacer unas casas en lo mejor de esta ciudad. . . . Haré matar todos mis parientes"'" ("First I will build some houses in the best part of the city. . . . I will have all my relatives killed"). He will erase all trace of family, the character tells us, so that people "'no sepan mi linaje'" (will not know my lin-eage).[16] Quevedo, in his *Libro de todas las cosas,* gives precise instructions for passing as an Old Christian: "'Para ser caballero o hidalgo, aunque seas judío y moro, haz mala letra, habla despacio y recio, anda a caballo, debe mucho, y vete donde no te conozcan, y lo serás'" (In order to be a knight or *hidalgo,* even if you are a Jew and a Moor, write poorly, speak slowly and loudly, ride on horseback, owe a lot, and go where no one knows you, and you will be one).[17] The context of dissimulation and impersonation that these authors parody necessarily colors the prolonged disguise of the *Persiles*'s wandering protago-nists and Clodio's insistence on exposing it.

Are there any alternatives to the search for origins? Prince Arnaldo provides the perfect foil for Clodio, his would-be counselor, by resolutely refusing to inquire into Auristela's past. From the very beginning he insists that her lineage does not interest him. He stresses instead what her own person reveals about her:

—Nunca quise saber más de su hacienda de aquello que ella quiso decirme, pintándola en mi imaginación, no como persona ordinaria y de bajo estado, sino como reina de todo el mundo, porque su honestidad, su gravedad, su discreción tan en estremo estremada, no me daba lugar a que otra cosa pensase. . . . Jamás me quiso decir su calidad ni la de sus padres, ni yo, como ya he dicho, le importuné me la dijese, pues ella sola, por sí misma, sin que traiga dependencia de otra alguna nobleza, merece, no solamente la corona de Dinamarca, sino de toda la monarquía de la tierra. (124)

"I never tried to find out more about her [wealth] than she chose to tell me, picturing her in my imagination not as a common person of low estate but as the queen of the whole world, for her modesty, her dignified manner, and her extraordinarily extraordinary mind wouldn't let me think anything else. . . . She never consented to tell me her social rank or that of her parents, nor did I, as I've said, beg her to tell me; for she alone, just for herself, with no need of any other nobility, deserves not only the crown of Denmark, but that of the whole world." (72–73)

The modern reader's impatience with Auristela's impossible perfection, as described in these paeans, has somewhat obscured the significance of Arnaldo's indifference to her origins. In fact, he embraces her deracinated, mysterious person with no concern for the truth. Periandro assures him that Auristela is "de ilustrísimo linaje nacida" (125) ("born of a very illustrious family line" [73]) but simultaneously asks that Arnaldo not force him to tell lies by inquiring further, to which request the courteous Arnaldo acquiesces. His curiosity makes him listen to Clodio, but as soon as the *maldiciente* has his say, Arnaldo rejects his insinuations in no uncertain terms: "—Auristela es buena, Periandro es su hermano, y yo no quiero creer otra cosa, porque ella ha dicho que lo es" (175) ("'Auristela is good, Periandro is her brother, and I don't want to believe anything else, for she's said it's so'" [113]). As Sancho might point out, "No hay peor sordo que el que no quiere oír."

Constantly portrayed as a reasonable character, Arnaldo is no fool blinded by love; instead, he exercises a particular decorum with respect to his beloved's lineage. After following Auristela and Periandro all the way to Rome, he insists that he is not interested in her wealth or blood but will take her "sin otra dote que la grande que ella tiene en su virtud y hermosura" (430) ("with no other dowry but the large one she brings in her virtue and beauty" [314]). He expresses the Neoplatonic conviction that nobility accompanies natural excellence:

no quiero averiguar la nobleza de su linaje, pues está claro que no había de negar naturaleza los bienes de la fortuna a quien tantos dio de sí misma. Nunca en humildes sujetos, o pocas veces, hace su asiento virtudes grandes, y la belleza del cuerpo muchas veces es indicio de la belleza del alma. (430)

Nor do I want to investigate the nobility of her [lineage], for it's clear Nature wouldn't deny worldly goods to someone she'd endowed so bountifully with her own natural gifts. Never, or very rarely, do high virtues find a place in lowborn people, and the beauty of the body is often an indication of the beauty of the soul. (314)

Although Arnaldo's emphasis on the correlation between nobility and virtue might seem reactionary, there is a certain defiance in his dismissal of lineage to focus on the individual subject. The conviction that descendants should pay for the taint of their forebears was one of the most controversial aspects of the *limpieza* investigations.[18] From this perspective, Arnaldo's paradoxical emphasis on an innate nobility that resides in the individual subject suddenly appears far more radical. His refusal to investigate stems from this conviction: Auristela's nobility is, to him, self-apparent.[19]

Clodio, by comparison, remains convinced that the heroine is passing herself off as noble despite murky origins. His suspicion clarifies what is surely one of the oddest turns in the narrative: his attempt to win Auristela for himself. He writes her a letter stressing her own victimization and his resourcefulness, explicitly touting his ability "para saber vivir en los más últimos rincones de la tierra" (190) ("to live in the farthest corners of the earth" [126]). The none-too-subtle implication is that Auristela's wanderings with Periandro will have no end and that she will be better off picking a resourceful man who might help her avoid so many shipwrecks and pirates. Clodio's matter-of-fact yet outrageous offer is tantamount to shouting, "The Emperor has no clothes!"—it forces us to realize how flimsy is our own sense of Auristela's identity or purpose. With impeccable timing the text then somewhat counters Clodio's accusations by providing, for the first time, the protagonists' true names, if not their lineage (185–86).

Meanwhile, Clodio's denunciations bring swift retribution. Before the outraged Auristela can punish him for his daring proposal, he is shot through the mouth with an arrow by the young *bárbaro* Antonio—"el pez por la boca muere." The peculiar staging of Clodio's death at Policarpo's court brings the problems of contemporary Spain much closer. Antonio's wayward arrow was actually intended for the Moorish witch Cenotia, an exile from Spain, who had been attempting to seduce him. Although Cenotia is certainly not a sympathetic character, her account of her suffering and escape from Spain suggests the very real costs and consequences of inquisitorial zeal:

—la persecución de los que llaman inquisidores en España, me arrancó de mi patria; que cuando se sale por fuerza della, antes se puede llamar arrancada que salida. Vine a esta isla por estraños rodeos, por infinitos peligros, casi siempre como si estuvieran cerca, volviendo la cabeza atrás, pensando que me mordían las faldas los perros. (202)

"persecution in Spain by those known as Inquisitors tore me from my homeland, for when one is forced to leave it, [it's more being torn away than simply gone]. I came to this island by strange roundabout ways, through countless dangers, [almost always turning my head back as though they were near, thinking the dogs were nipping at my skirts]." (135)

Cenotia's highly compressed account shares the *estraños rodeos* and *infinitos peligros* of Auristela and Periandro's narrative; unlike their story, however, the *mise-en-abîme* frankly states origins. Cenotia moves quickly from her beginnings to her desperate love for Antonio and rises to embrace him. He attempts to shoot her but instead kills Clodio, who is just entering the room. The compressed scene has the flavor of a morality play, staging an implicit battle between Inquisitional zeal and marginalized subjects. The exiled Cenotia is spared while the *maldiciente* Clodio is summarily silenced. In case we have missed the point, the narrator stresses Antonio's *felix culpa*, telling us that he unwittingly "acertó errando" (204) (that is, "he hit the mark by mistake" [136]).

The next stage of Cenotia's story provides an oblique commentary on the racialized persecution of Spain's religious others. Scorned, she avenges herself by casting spells on Antonio until his father irately demands that she remove them and restore him to health.[20] The exchange with Antonio senior—*el bárbaro español*—blatantly emphasizes his Spanishness over any barbarian qualities: he pounces on Cenotia "con cólera española y discurso ciego" (217) ("full of Spanish fury and blind rage" [146]; she trembles "en las manos de un español colérico" (218) ("in the hands of an enraged Spaniard" [146]) and addresses him as such. As she pleads for mercy for those who have surrendered, the languages of erotic and of military conquest become indistinguishable: "—Suéltame, español, y envaina tu acero, que los que tiene tu hijo le han conducido al término en que está. . . . Aconséjale que se humane de aquí en adelante con los rendidos, y no menosprecie a los que piedad le pidieren" (218) ("'Let me go, Spaniard, and sheathe your steel, for it was your son's steely heart that got him into this present mess. . . . Advise him to act in the future with more humane compassion for those who surrender to him, and not to show contempt for those who beg him for mercy'" [146]).[21]

The suddenly most Spanish Antonio takes her point: addressing his son, he transforms Cenotia's pleas for mercy into a frankly Erasmian homily on gently instructing those who offend instead of militantly repressing them. His holy law, he insists,

—nos enseña que no estamos obligados a castigar a los que nos ofenden, sino a aconsejarlos la enmienda de sus delitos. . . . Cuando te convidaren a hacer ofensas que redunden en deservicio de Dios, no tienes para qué armar el arco, ni disparar flechas, ni decir injuriosas palabras: que, con no recibir el consejo y apartarte de la ocasión, quedarás vencedor de la pelea. (219)

"teaches us we shouldn't punish those who offend us, rather counsel them to mend their ways. . . . Whenever someone tempts you to commit offenses that may lead to the disservice of God, you'll have no reason to arm your bow, nor to shoot arrows, nor to use insults, for simply by not accepting the offer and escaping from the situation you'll turn out to be the winner in the struggle." (147)

In a marked departure from the inquisitorial approach to heterodoxy within Spain, Antonio discounts the threat of the ungodly. Sinfulness, he suggests, is not contagious—the only response it requires is peaceful refusal. His emphasis on full agency and measured exchanges between conscious actors strikes a very different note from the metaphors of communicable disease often used to describe the Semitic or heretical presence within Spain.[22] Thus the chastisement of the Moorish witch by the *bárbaro español* becomes instead a plea for tolerance, or at least for Christian moderation.

In an ironic twist, Cenotia herself seems unable to read the allegory of Clodio's death and deliberately takes on the role of suspicious counselor. Whereas Clodio had attempted to warn Prince Arnaldo, Cenotia whispers in King Policarpo's ear that Auristela and Periandro's relationship is not what it seems. She gives terrible counsel, suggesting that Policarpo kidnap Auristela and Antonio and scare the others away. The plan fails miserably and Cenotia is murdered by the rebellious mob that also deposes the unjust ruler (252). Yet before meeting with an ostensibly fitting end for a Moorish witch, Cenotia mobilizes a series of crucial issues—dissimulation versus exposure, tolerance versus persecution, Christian forbearance versus militant repression—that complicate the conventionality of her character.

Clodio, Arnaldo, and Cenotia provide different perspectives on the examination of lineage and the appropriate reaction to its disclosure. Their sustained concern with either investigating or pointedly not investigating the protagonists constantly recalls the fact that Periandro and Auristela are not who they say they are. Yet the text clearly valorizes the deliberate opacity of their self-presentation over the desire for transparency and revelation, even though the doubts that Clodio and Cenotia voice are more than justified. The exaltation of characters whose true identity remains hidden until the very end—despite the many questions raised about them—provides a literary alternative to the societal obsession with genealogical purity. In the *Persiles,* identity is deliberately disguised, and that disguise is deliberately sustained, despite the zeal of *maldicientes* and the reader's own curiosity. Through its constant digressions and critique of transparency, the text proposes alternative forms of reading pleasure that do not depend on unmasking and revelation but rather on proliferating stories and sustained impersonation.

Byzantine Wanderings

The storm- and pirate-driven progress of the *Persiles,* especially in its first half, proclaims its debt to the Byzantine novel. Touting his forthcoming book to readers in the prologue to the *Novelas ejemplares,* Cervantes describes it as a "libro que se atreve a competir con Heliodoro, si ya por atrevido no sale con las manos en la cabeza" (1.53) (a book that dares to compete with Heliodorus, if it doesn't come out with its hands on its head for its daring). The arrogant claim to outdo a model—Heliodorus's *Aethiopica*—gives way to a more complex acknowledgment that the text's soundness may in fact be compromised. As Diana de Armas Wilson points out, "con las manos en la cabeza" means "injured or battered."[23] But what kind of daring would threaten the wholeness of the *Persiles* in these terms? As I suggest above, the text's *atrevimiento* is both formal and ideological, for it erects the preservation of the protagonists' secret into a narrative principle. Yet the explicit claim of a Byzantine lineage suggests that the *Persiles*'s daring is at least partially connected to the specific possibilities of the genre and to its riskier transformations.

The Byzantine novel became an increasingly respected genre over the course of the sixteenth century, with the third-century *Aethiopica,* rediscovered in 1526, praised most highly.[24] Heliodorus's novel was especially popular in Erasmian circles: the first translation into Spanish was published in Ambères in 1554 by an anonymous *secreto amigo de la patria* (secret friend of his native land)—presumably an Erasmian exiled from Spain. Cervantes was probably most familiar with the immensely popular 1587 translation by Fernando de Mena, the *Historia etiópica de los amores de Teágenes y Cariclea,* published in Alcalá de Henares.

As Constance Rose suggests, the Byzantine novel, with its repeated emphasis on Mediterranean wanderings and disguised identity, is markedly apposite to the experience of marginalized and persecuted exiles from early modern Spain. In her study of the exile Alonso Núñez de Reinoso, she argues that "the rediscovery and vogue for the Byzantine novel among intellectuals may be interpreted, in part, as a means of expressing enforced exile, with the concomitant of endless wandering and travail."[25] Although Rose's account of the connection between the early modern predilection for Byzantine novels and the expulsion of the Jews from Spain is at times reductive, it does suggest a powerful way to rethink the genre in historical and ideological terms.

Cervantes acknowledges only Heliodorus as his Byzantine model, yet critics have demonstrated his familiarity also with Núñez de Reinoso's *Historia de los amores de Clareo y Florisea y de los trabajos de la sin ventura Isea*, published in Venice at the heart of a Jewish circle in 1552.[26] I am less interested here in rehearsing the similarities between *Clareo and Florisea* and the *Persiles* than in exploring the more unusual features of Reinoso's text and their elaboration in Cervantes. Reinoso's idiosyncratic transformation of Achilles Tatius's *Clitophon and Leucippe* constitutes a fascinating precedent for the *Persiles* precisely in the ways it departs from the Byzantine novel to incorporate contemporary issues.

To the traditional dyad of faithful, chaste lovers separated by multiple adventures, Reinoso adds a third character: the narrator, Isea, whose own miseries far outlast the lovers' reunion. Humiliated by Clareo's rejection of her and her unwitting adultery, Isea must leave her home in Ephesus to go "por el mundo a vivir y morar en estranjeras y peregrinas tierras" (off into the world to live in foreign and strange lands).[27] After a series of both Byzantine and chivalric adventures and a Virgilian visit to the underworld, Isea suddenly lands in a far less fanciful Spain. In an episode whose satirical thrust was recognized by both Menéndez Pelayo and Bataillon, Isea attempts to enter a convent that discriminates according to both wealth and *limpieza:* "la abadesa me respondió que yo fuese bien venida; pero que cuanto a entrar en aquella casa, que era menester traer mil ducados de dote, y ser de don y de buen linaje; porque todas aquellas señoras lo eran" (467) (the abbess answered that I was welcome but that, as for joining that house, it was necessary to bring a dowry of one thousand *ducados* and to be of the nobility and of good lineage, because all those ladies were).

While the ladies beat each other with their *chapines* in a quarrel over who has the most august lineage, Isea, "viendo aquella quistion y que no tenia dineros para entrar allí, ni menos se podia saber quien era" (467) (seeing this issue and that she had no money to enter there, much less could anyone know who she was), leaves Spain for the refuge of the Insula Pastoril, or Pastoral Isle, from which she narrates her story. Yet it is a Spanish audience that she specifically longs for as she concludes her story in self-imposed exile,

engañando mis trabajos con lo que escribo, como hace la doncella las largas noches con la tarea, viviendo aquí sin ser usada a estos cielos, ni a las aguas, ni manjares destas tierras; sin tener persona ninguna a quien pueda contar mis males, ni con quien descanse en mis trabajos. . . . Bien sé que si esta mi obra en algún tiempo aportare a las riberas del rio Henares, que piadosamente será leida, y mis penas sentidas y con razon lloradas. (467–68)

[disguising my troubles with what I write, as does the damsel with her needlework on long nights, living here but not used to these skies nor to the waters nor the foods of these lands; without a single person to whom I might tell my misfortunes, nor with whom I might rest in my troubles. . . . I well know that if ever I should take this my work to the shores of the Henares (near Guadalajara, and the famous university of Alcalá de Henares), it will be read with pity, and my sorrows felt and wept for with good reason.]

Here, at the end of Isea's narrative, her repeated complaints about her wanderings and misfortunes give way to a far more direct lament for Spain. The clear and yet geographically incongruous yearning in this passage strongly suggests Reinoso's longing for his own unattainable homeland. With its echo of the nymph Elisa, from Garcilaso de la Vega's "Egloga III," ". . . y lleva presuroso / al mar de Lusitania el nombre mío / donde será escuchado, yo lo fío" (and swiftly takes my name to the Lusitanian sea where, I warrant, it will be heard),[28] written while the poet was in Naples, Isea's lament combines poetic and biographical allusions. While Rose's attempt to read Isea's story as a roman à clef, with thinly veiled references to Reinoso's travels and patrons, seems somewhat literal-minded, her careful contextualization of the heroine's laments and the theme of adverse fortune with respect to contemporary *converso* experience is highly persuasive.[29] Hence, even if we do not accept the one-to-one correspondences that Rose suggests, Reinoso's transformation of the Byzantine novel into a capacious fictionalization of the sorrows of exile and exclusion appears incontrovertible. With the *Historia de los amores de Clareo y Florisea y de los trabajos de la sin ventura Isea,* the Byzantine novel undergoes a formal and thematic transformation that radically modernizes it, bringing within its purview both the chivalric and pastoral genres and the ideological questions that so exercised Cervantes and his contemporaries.

Peregrinations

My own reading of the influence of Isea's *trabajos* on Cervantes's *Los trabajos de Persiles y Sigismunda,* focuses on the latter's broad concern with wandering versus inclusion rather than on specific correspondences in text or context. That is, I am not interested in demonstrating that Periandro and Auristela's travels are an allegory for the Second Diaspora or that their reticence marks them as *conversos*—although both are intriguing, if far-fetched, possibilities.

Instead, what concerns me is how Cervantes, as a sympathetic reader of Isea's exile, charts a centripetal movement from the far confines of the northern world to Rome, concluding his own narrative of sorrowful wandering with a broad welcome into the fold of the Church and into a metaphorical and universalized Spain. This trajectory from exclusion to inclusion powerfully reimagines the discriminatory and repressive practices of Cervantes's Spain, replacing them with a generous confidence in the perfectibility of religious practice. To be sure, there are limits to the inclusion: the Roman interlude includes the stereotypical Jew Zabulón and his wife, a witch who poisons Auristela, robbing her of her beauty. This Jew recalls the Moor Cenotia, who is also reprised in the episode of the treacherous Moriscos in book III, chapter 11. None of these marginalized characters benefit from the capacious Christianity that Cervantes imagines, although, as I suggest in the case of Cenotia, a closer look at their presentation often reveals a devastating irony.

As Auristela and Periandro make their way to Rome, the text insists on the ambiguity of their motivations. At the dangerous court of King Policarpo, Auristela tests Periandro by offering to release him from their dangerous *peregrinación*: "—Fuera estamos de nuestra patria, tú perseguido de tu hermano, y yo de mi corta suerte. Nuestro camino a Roma cuanto más le procuramos, más se dificulta y alarga" (177) ("'We're away from our homeland, you're pursued by your brother and I by my bad luck. The more we try to follow our road to Rome, the more difficult and longer it becomes'" [115]). Auristela's choice of words to describe their travails is striking: the characters will eventually pass as pilgrims but are not actually on a pilgrimage. The proleptic term acquires here the etymological meaning that Rose associates with Reinoso and the *converso* experience—that of wandering through a strange land.[30] The pilgrims are never referred to as *romeros* or as being on *romería*—the terms for "pilgrim" and "pilgrimage" that are etymologically connected to Rome. Far from a simple teleological quest, their *peregrinación* bears a complex, multilayered relationship to its putative religious ends.

Upon their arrival in Portugal, Auristela immediately seeks out, with true pilgrim zeal, the monastery of Belén: "quiso Auristela, enamorada y devota de la fama de aquel santo monasterio, visitarle primero, y adorar en él al verdadero Dios libre y desembarazadamente, sin las torcidas ceremonias de su tierra" (278) ("Auristela, feeling love and devotion for the fame of that holy monastery, wanted to visit it first and there worship the one true God, freely and unhindered by the warped rites of her land" [195]). Whatever *torcidas ceremonias* Auristela may be trying to straighten out, Periandro still conceives of pilgrimage as a pragmatic disguise. Immediately following, he suggests that the travelers dress as pilgrims to avoid unwanted attention, as one more measure to protect their secret:

lleváronlos al gobernador, que, después de admirado de verlos, no se cansaba de
preguntarles quiénes eran, de dónde venían y adónde iban. A lo que respondió
Periandro, que ya traía estudiada la respuesta que había de dar a semejantes pre-
guntas, viendo que se le habían de hacer muchas veces: cuando quería o le parecía que le convenía, relataba su historia a lo largo, encubriendo siempre sus padres de modo que, satisfaciendo a los que le preguntaban, en breves razones
cifraba, si no toda, a lo menos gran parte de su historia. . . . fue parecer de Periandro mudasen los trajes de bárbaros en los de peregrinos, porque la novedad
de los que traían era la causa principal de ser tan seguidos, que ya parecían per-
seguidos del vulgo; además, que para el viaje que ellos llevaban de Roma, nin-
guno les venía más a cuento. Hízose así, y de allí a dos días se vieron peregrinamente peregrinos. (279)

they were taken to the governor who, after his initial amazement on seeing them,
never tired of asking who they were, where they came from, and where they were
going. Periandro responded to all that, for he'd already thought through the
answers to be given to such questions, knowing they'd be put to them often. When
he wanted to, or whenever it seemed to his advantage, he told his story from
beginning to end (always concealing who his parents were), [so that, satisfying
those who asked, he briefly enciphered, if not all, then at least the greater part of
his story]. . . . Periandro felt it best for them to change their barbarian clothes
for those of pilgrims, for the novelty of the ones they were wearing was the principal cause of their being hounded, and indeed, it seemed as though they were
actually being pursued by the rabble; besides, no clothing would be more appropriate for the journey they were taking to Rome. [They did so, and in two days
wondrously found themselves pilgrims.] (196)

There is a nice irony in a convenient disguise that *venía a cuento*—suited the
occasion—but also complements Periandro's ciphered tales. These pilgrims
become who they are *peregrinamente*—rarely or wondrously—as their disguise
rids them of the marks of otherness and affords them a relative anonymity.
The irony seems even more marked as the new pilgrims set off for Rome "con
licencia del virrey y con patentes verdaderas y firmes de quiénes eran y adónde
iban" (282) ("with permission from the viceroy and with [true] documents
attesting to and authenticating who they were and where they were going"
[198]). What can these documents possibly say when the protagonists' identity remains concealed?

The so-called pilgrims' deliberate and partial self-construction in book III
for the benefit of Portuguese and Spanish authorities is thematized in their
encounters with various other kinds of artistic and theatrical representations,
from the canvas that Periandro paints to avoid telling and retelling the story
(282) to the dramatist who envisions Auristela as a cross-dressed actress and
imagines writing a *comedia* based on her story (284–85).[31] The protagonists'

disguise contributes to the general sense of disorder that characterizes Spain in the text. The officers of the Santa Hermandad, for example, take them for murderers: although they falsely accuse them of hiding crimes under a cloak of Christian virtue, they underscore the multiple possible motivations for the pilgrims' garb (302).

The prolonged ambiguity regarding the pilgrims' motivation and authenticity makes their religious experience in Rome even more striking. Auristela deflates Periandro's excitement as they near the end of their journey by recalling their displacement: "—Lejos nos hallamos de nuestras tierras, no conocidos de nadie en las ajenas, sin arrimo que sustente la yedra de nuestras incomodidades" (414) ("'We're far from our own lands, known by no one in these foreign ones, with no support to which we can cling like ivy amidst our hardships'" [302]). Yet the Church offers her a refuge, as she is instructed in "todo aquello que a ella le parecía que le faltaba por saber de la fe católica; a lo menos, de aquello que en su patria escuramente se platicaba" (435) ("everything she felt she needed to know about the Catholic faith, [or at least about what was practiced darkly in her homeland]" [318–19]). This introduction to the very long litany of what Auristela learns is truly remarkable, both for its insistence on her own volition and self-determination in seeking the true faith and for the absence of any prejudice against her for past murky practices. In a striking contrast to the Spanish polity, the Roman Church that Cervantes envisions here is wide open to those who seek entry, whatever their pasts. The instruction of Auristela echoes the conversion of Ricla the barbarian in book I—a conversion fully achieved, Ricla maintains, despite the absence of the ceremonies used in Spain (82). The two scenes of Christianization—of the more clearly marked barbarian and of the ignorant pilgrim Auristela—mark the *Persiles*'s solution to the wanderings and trials of its protagonists: inclusion in a welcoming and broadly conceived community of the faith.

Periandro's own experiences in Rome suggest that the religious openness of the last book has its equivalent in the political register. He is repeatedly taken for a Spaniard, first by a Spanish messenger (432), whom he corrects, and then by a Roman courtesan—ironically named Hipólita—and her pimp (443–44), to whom he replies as a Spaniard. The latter two associate Spanishness with excess, foolhardy arrogance, and manliness: the courtesan embraces Periandro, to see "si son tan valientes los españoles como tienen fama" (445) ("if Spaniards are as brave as their reputation" [326]). Periandro first corrects her by emphasizing his pilgrim costume over his supposed national identity: "—los peregrinos, aunque sean españoles, no están obligados a ser valientes" (445) ("'pilgrims, even though they may be Spaniards, aren't required to be brave'" [326]); then he fully takes on a Spanish identity only to challenge the stereotype of martial virility: "—Aunque soy español, soy algún tanto medroso, y más os temo a vos sola que a un ejército de enemigos" (445) ("'Although I'm a Spaniard, I'm somewhat cowardly and more afraid of you by yourself than a whole army of enemies'" [326]). In refusing the sinful advances of Hipólita, Periandro acts out the recommendation on proper Spanish behavior—composed refusal—that the elder Antonio had given his son when Cenotia pursued him. More important, he fashions himself into a Spaniard while insisting on his peaceable Christian virtue. As in the echo of Ricla's conversion in Auristela's instruction, Periandro's story here reprises the barbarian's even as it broadens the inclusiveness of the text from religious to national categories. All it takes for the wanderer Periandro to pass as a Spaniard is to become complicit in the confusion of those who take him for one.

Inclusion within Spain seems less available to the Moriscos depicted in book III, chapter 11. The pilgrims arrive at a small coastal town in Spain where there are almost no Old Christians. The Morisca Rafala, a true Christian, warns them that all the townspeople plan to escape to North Africa on corsair ships and advises them to seek refuge in the town church with her uncle Jarife, "moro solo en el nombre, y en las obras cristiano" (355) ("a Moor in name only, and a Christian in his deeds" [255]). Jarife then voices a hyperstereotypical denunciation of the Moriscos, so clichéd and virulent as to advertise its own artificiality, much like Ricote's ironic praise for the 1609 expulsion of the Moriscos from Spain in part II of *Don Quijote*. Jarife announces, "—Morisco soy, señores, y ojalá que negarlo pudiera, pero no por esto dejo de ser cristiano" (356) ("'I'm a Morisco, señores, though I wish I could deny it, but that doesn't keep me from being a Christian'" [255–56]), and longs for a brave king who will dare to expel his people. He reassures this imaginary sovereign that he must not fear the depopulation and ruin of Morisco lands, for "con los nuevos cristianos viejos que esta tierra se poblare, se volverá a fertilizar, y a poner en mucho mejor punto que agora tiene" (356) ("the new old Christians will populate this land and it will once again become productive and even more fertile than now" [256]). But by the time the *Persiles* was written, the dire economic effects of the expulsion had become obvious; and since even sincere Christians like Jarife had been expelled, there was no one to occupy the paradoxical category of *nuevo cristiano viejo*.[32] Thus this exclusionary interlude actually evinces the costs of the Morisco expulsion while adding the sympathetic figures of Rafala and Jarife to the Cervantine roster of most Christian Moriscos that already includes Ricote and his daughter, Ana Félix.

In his important work resituating the *Persiles* in the context of the Spanish Empire, George Mariscal argues for the central role of the barbarian Antonio and his family, suggesting that they mark the way that "new world cultures had problematized the traditional oppositions that governed Spanish thinking."[33] His discussion of the gradual and remarkable inclusion of the mestizo children of Antonio and Ricla gets at one of the fundamental contradictions of early modern Spain: "To what extent could traditional Spanish society, which was constructed upon a series of exclusions and issues of blood purity, to what extent could this Spain accommodate the 'new' peoples born of the contact with indigenous groups in America?"[34] Ricla and her children, who appear to be perfectly assimilated into European society, seem to be perfect examples of the phenomenon of "racial drift" that I describe in chapter 1. As I show in this chapter, the *Persiles*'s concern with inclusion goes far beyond the incorporation of the barbarian to encompass dubious wanderers of unknown origin. Its inclusion of northern heretics who recall the *converso* plight seems at least as remarkable as its recuperation of barbarians. With its critique of transparency, its emphasis on a welcoming Church, and its flexible version of Spanish identity, the *Persiles* challenges any conclusive categorization of subjects, suggesting instead that identity and allegiance are both malleable and perfectible.

"La española inglesa": A Mirror across the Water

As Rafael Lapesa pointed out long ago, there are multiple similarities between the *Persiles* and Cervantes's "English" novella: both tell of a pair of idealized lovers who finally marry after numerous adventures and delays and after reaffirming their Catholic faith.[35] Yet the connections between the two texts go beyond the Counter-Reformation topoi of spiritual development. With its emphasis on paradoxical, highly unstable identities, "La española inglesa" translates the *Persiles*'s concern with passing and inclusion to a Protestant context hostile to Catholicism. Central elements of the *Persiles* read differently when reflected and refracted in this mirror image: the simultaneous duplication of narrative elements and transformation of their context both fleshes out and alters their significance.

Carroll B. Johnson marvelously grounds the story of Isabela, a Spanish merchant's daughter captured during the raid of Cádiz, and her Catholic English lover, Ricaredo, within the economic and political realities of the early seventeenth century.[36] He argues that, far from being an idealistic romance, "La española inglesa" engages with pressing class issues of feudalism versus capitalism and aristocrats versus an emerging bourgeoisie. My own brief reading of the novella in light of the *Persiles* stresses, first, its implicit critique of the Spanish obsession with religious transparency and, second, its complication of national versus religious allegiances.

As Américo Castro points out, the England Cervantes imagines in "La española inglesa" is ruled by a remarkably tolerant sovereign, one who not only suffers but favors Catholics.[37] When Isabela is introduced to her royal namesake, the girl's recusant adoptive family trembles at their imminent exposure. But the queen, informed of Isabela's stubborn *católico intento* (Catholic intent), states that "por eso la estimaba en más, pues tan bien sabía guardar la ley que sus padres la habían enseñado" (268) (she esteemed her all the more for that, for she so followed the faith her parents had taught her). Isabela's identity is in fact a palimpsest: the queen's reference to genealogy recalls that, within a Spanish context, a rich merchant's daughter would be ostracized as a New Christian.[38] Yet in England, where Catholics are generally persecuted for their adherence to the faith of their fathers, she is taken for a full-fledged Catholic, and her allegiance to the Church is never questioned. Thus the irony of the novella functions at several different levels. First, the passing recusants in England are presented as the other side of the coin to the persecuted New Christians in Spain. As Manuel da Costa Fontes cogently points out, the crucial difference is that "to Cervantes's contemporaries, those who remained faithful to Catholicism in England deserved praise."[39] Second, a *conversa* is constructed into an exemplary Catholic in the eyes of Catholicism's enemies, suggesting that only within the borders of Spain is religious allegiance perceived to depend on lineage. In Spain, Isabela would not be accepted as a Catholic even if she claimed to be one; in England, she is identified as such even when she presumably attempts to hide her religion. The queen's refusal to persecute Isabela for her dissimulation resonates with Arnaldo's reluctance to investigate Auristela's secrets in the *Persiles*. In both cases concealment is explicitly valorized over transparency; beyond the borders of Spain, the texts suggest, the inquisitorial impulse appears to be fundamentally misguided.

In this sense, both "La española inglesa" and the *Persiles* value surface over depth. The apparent allegiance of Isabela and her adoptive family to the queen is enough; the sovereign feels no need to root out their secret sympathies or to reveal a traitorous essence, although she will test Ricaredo through his actions.[40] Similarly, Arnaldo trusts Auristela's surface and refuses to go beyond it. Strikingly, both sovereigns have good reason to be worried—Isabela is a Catholic; Auristela is not, in fact, Periandro's sister—yet the texts clearly privilege constructed, even artificial identities over the search for authenticity. The parallel episodes of poisoning in the *Persiles* and "La española inglesa" become quite interesting when read in this light. In each case, when the heroine is poisoned she does not die but instead loses all her beauty. The hero then proves the magnitude of his love by remaining loyal to her and is rewarded with her return to her original state. The poison thus appears analogous to Clodio's inquiring gaze: it penetrates the beauteous surface to reveal an ugliness beneath. The lovers' loyalty to their disfigured ladies, which they themselves gloss as an attachment to their souls (depth) over their bodies (surface), may also be read as the opposite, that is, as a refusal to privilege the revealed core over the destroyed surface. The memory of whatever selves Auristela and Isabela had presented to the world is more powerful than what the poison discloses beneath them.

Ricaredo, for his own part, must struggle to reconcile his religious and national allegiances in the face of widespread suspicion. Required by the queen to prove himself worthy of Isabela, he becomes a privateer, albeit one with a conscience:

> Ricaredo se hizo a la vela, combatido, entre otros muchos, de dos pensamientos que le tenían fuera de sí: era el uno considerar que le convenía hacer hazañas que le hiciesen merecedor de Isabela, y el otro, que no podía hacer ninguna, si había de responder a su católico intento, que le impedía no desenvainar la espada contra católicos; y si no la desenvainaba, había de ser notado de cristiano o de cobarde, y todo esto redundaba en perjuicio de su vida y en obstáculo de su pretensión. Pero, en fin, determinó de posponer al gusto de enamorado el que tenía de ser católico, y en su corazón pedía al cielo le deparase ocasiones donde, con ser valiente, cumpliese con ser cristiano, dejando a su reina satisfecha y a Isabel merecida. (252)

> [Ricaredo set sail, torn by two thoughts, among many others, that left him beside himself: one was to consider that he ought to do deeds worthy of Isabela; the other, that he could do none if he were to follow his Catholic leanings, which forbade him to draw his sword against Catholics. And if he didn't he would be seen as a Christian or a coward, and all this would threaten his life and get in the way of his suit. At last he determined to postpone to his lover's delight the delight he had in being Catholic, and in his heart he begged Heaven to give him opportunities to be both brave and a proper Christian so as to satisfy his queen and merit Isabela.]

The confusion between Catholicism and Christianity in this passage suggests the complexity of Ricaredo's choices. The grammatical obfuscation—he postpones his religious duty for the sake of his love, but the sentence structure suggests the opposite—reflects the difficulty of his situation. In response to his plea, Heaven sends Ricaredo two Turkish ships escorting a rich Portuguese prize: this common enemy to Catholics and Protestants solves Ricaredo's dilemma. The Turks, lured by the false Spanish flags that the English fly as they pass collectively, "por desmentir a quien llegase a reconocellos, y no los tuviese por navíos de cosarios" (253) (to fool anyone who might recognize them and so that they would not be taken for pirates), attack the English and are promptly defeated. Ricaredo decides to free the Spanish galley slaves, yet his mercy makes him suspect, so that he must free a few Turks for good measure (258). With a little help from Providence, Ricaredo successfully challenges the notion of a perfect correspondence between religious and national allegiances: his compassion toward fellow Catholics in no way harms his sovereign's interests, and he sails for home with the rich prize in tow.

As though to underscore the apparent irreconcilability of his identity, Ricaredo returns to London as a kind of emblem of contradiction. His ship is decorated with conflicting banners; his own cosmopolitan attire includes Milanese armor and Swiss breeches. His appearance even contravenes gender norms, suggesting a highly stylized cross-dressing to match his crossing of religious and national lines: "Con el paso brioso que llevaba, algunos hubo que le compararon a Marte, dios de las batallas, y otros, llevados de la hermosura de su rostro, dicen que le compararon a Venus, que para hacer alguna burla a Marte de aquel modo se había disfrazado" (259) (With his spirited gait, some compared him to Mars, god of war, while others, moved by the beauty of his visage, were said to have compared him to Venus, who had thus dressed up to play some trick on Mars).[41] Yet this undecidability in no way affects Ricaredo's relation with his sovereign: he remains an exemplary, though contradictory, subject—a fit captain for English ships flying Spanish flags.

The separation of religious and national allegiance in the novella radically breaks with the Spanish model of a perfect correspondence between faith and national identity to suggest—in the mirror image of Cervantes's England—the possibility of a heterogeneous polity. The force of this vision is somewhat attenuated by the resolution, which brings the Catholic Englishman to Spain. Ricaredo's relocation is, however, purely voluntary as he rejoins Isabela in Seville. Although welcome, he remains a foreigner: his fairness marks his difference, and Isabela must translate for him (277, 279). His heterogeneity is as marked in his new home as in his country of origin, yet it does not impede his existence within either.

Ricaredo's trajectory from England to Spain again recalls the *Persiles:* like Periandro and Auristela, he escapes an undesirable marriage with the excuse of a voyage to Rome and then carries out his religious intent. In the Holy City, Ricaredo undergoes a *reducción,* or formal reconciliation with the Church that erases any lingering doubts about his religious conviction: "—confesé mis pecados con el mayor penitenciero, absolvióme dellos, y diome los recaudos necesarios que diesen fe de mi confesión y penitencia y de la reducción que había hecho a nuestra universal madre la Iglesia" (279) ("I confessed my sins to the chief penitentiary, he absolved me of them and gave me the necessary documents to prove my confession and penitence and my reconciliation with our universal mother, the Church").[42] The formal *reducción* provides Ricaredo with proof of his adherence to the true faith and counteracts whatever dissimulation he had engaged in while in England. Yet while extolling a Catholic essence over the Protestant surface, the episode also suggests a straightforward and uncomplicated entry into the Church, even for as contradictory a subject as Ricaredo. Much like Auristela, he is welcomed into the fold regardless of his murky northern past, and the formal process that he undergoes clarifies the import of Auristela's theological instruction. In both cases the Church enables the transformation of subjects who leave behind previous selves to embrace an orthodox Christianity by adopting a new identity. The *reducción* thus paradoxically contributes to the process of manufacturing identity that is most often associated in these texts with a necessary and enabling dissimulation. Far from underwriting any genealogical or inherent notion of authenticity, the Church as Cervantes imagines it encourages a reconstructed faith that serves just as well as any original. In both texts the Roman interlude involves a self-motivated profession of Catholicism that also makes available to the protagonists a phantasmatic belonging within Spain. It renders moot the investigative energies of slanderers and curious bystanders by constructing a new and unimpeachable religious subject, regardless of origins. Ultimately, then, even the very seat of orthodoxy participates in what I describe as the critique of transparency to offer contradictory "Spanish" subjects capable of negotiating multiple allegiances.

Afterword:
Passing and the Arts of Subjectification

"Ever passed for something you're not?" With this simple advertisement in a Miami newspaper, artists Hillary Leone and Jennifer Macdonald collected hundreds of stories from individuals who considered passing to be a central part of their identity. They selected thirty representative narratives to create a video project entitled, quite simply, *Passing* (1996). In the piece, a group of people face the camera simultaneously on a divided video screen, as if in a police lineup or flip-book, to relate how they pass across multiple categories: race, nationality, ethnicity, religion, gender, and sexual orientation. As they speak, they each perform the same sequence of movements, suggesting a commonality that coexists, however uneasily, with their differences. While the subjects matter-of-factly narrate their passing—acts of impersonation that involve varying degrees of active dissimulation or misrecognition—the artists further complicate matters by uncoupling the video and audio tracks, so that the viewer must effectively construct a coherent subject out of disparate elements. The video thereby introduces a second level of ambiguity, as viewers haplessly attempt to confirm the subjects of the narratives to which they are listening. The very attempt forces the audience to recognize the ways in which we instinctively rely on stereotypes to distinguish one kind of person from another. As the piece reminds us, while stereotypes color our experience of identity, passing troubles any certainties that classification might afford.

Leone and Macdonald's video neatly encapsulates some of the key aspects of passing as a cultural and political strategy. The stories all come from Miami, one of the most diverse cities in the United States and part of this country's ever evolving and highly porous border with Latin America. Passing in this context often presents a challenge to both the internal and external boundaries of the nation-state. Moreover, the individual stories that make up the video suggest the instability of the categories through which we apprehend identity and the way in which narrative can itself alter them. There are multiple possible intersections among these categories, whether controlled by the subjects who pass or imposed upon them by the viewers. While some of these people relish passing for a certain race, for example, they do not always appreciate other qualities ascribed to them as a result. The piece also emphasizes how passing may counter and even appropriate stereotyping, transforming it from a tool of discrimination into an art of subjectification. The passing subjects actively intervene in the creation of their own identities, even if their agency is limited by the roles and categories that the culture makes available to them.

It is a common fallacy to suppose that such sophisticated maneuvers of subjectification, such performative identities, could only occur in our own postmodern time. While it is true that contemporary critical theorists—and artists—have made us newly aware of the complexity and performativity of identity, the phenomena they identify are not exclusively modern. As I suggest throughout this book, the pressures of nation-formation, imperial expansion, and religious upheavals in the early modern period led to elaborate negotiations of identity and belonging. The classifying manias that accompanied these large-scale transformations themselves engendered the necessity of subverting or transcending categories. From renegades in the Mediterranean, to religious dissidents throughout Europe, to racial drifters in the New World, early modern subjects turned to passing as a central strategy of subjectification and, indeed, survival.

Cervantes's complex literary representation of these strategies evinces the challenge that they mount to essentialized categories of belonging, most crucially to the Spanish nation. The public *mesa de trucos* that the author promises in the prologue to the *Novelas ejemplares* hosts a delicate game of action and reaction, disguise and discovery, repression and reprieve. My analysis focuses on Cervantes because of the irresistible doubleness of his own passing— the generic legerdemain as well as the cross-cultural transvestism that it frequently dissimulates. Given the critical tradition that has so often written Cervantes, and especially his "idealizing" texts, *out* of history, it seems crucial to establish how, through an astute and highly strategic use of literary conventionality, the author intervenes in pressing historical debates on identity and belonging.

Beyond my own focus on Cervantes, however, I want to offer the concept of passing as a powerful tool for much broader investigations in the early modern period. Even as it emphasizes how identity is socially constructed, passing serves to recognize the role of individual agency in that construction.

It thus seems particularly useful for analyzing the cruxes that historical subjects faced when fashioning their identity in repressive contexts, as well as for reconstructing the historical implications of literary disguise and impersonation. A careful reading of passing, I conjecture, could radically transform our understanding of the construction of recusant identities vis-à-vis the Protestant majority in England or, conversely, the various fraught incarnations of Protestant resistance to Counter-Reformation hegemony on the Continent. It could also help critics re-envision the relationship between foreigners and nationals, between colonial and metropolitan subjects—whether in the New World or in Old World colonies such as Ireland or, more generally, between marginal and normative subjects. Passing encourages us to consider anew the permeability and constructedness of all these categories—and the many spaces in between—not just in literary texts, but across a wide range of historical materials, as well as in theatrical performances where stage impersonations vividly enact the crisis of categories that passing so often represents. By highlighting individual agency as well as the contradictions of exclusionary policies, passing reminds us that, along with repressive categories, there have always existed sophisticated strategies for escaping categorization. Narratives of national or religious cohesion are surprisingly vulnerable to creative imitation. Both the early modern instances that I describe as well as the Cervantine impersonations that I trace throughout this book suggest that the most effective mode of resistance to orthodox ideologies of exclusion may often be the construction of alternative fictions of identity.

Notes

Chapter 1: Passing and the Fictions of Spanish Identity

1. On the Hapsburgs' conflation of religious and imperial ideologies, see Marie Tanner, *The Last Descendant of Aeneas: The Hapsburgs and the Mythic Image of the Emperor* (New Haven, Conn.: Yale University Press, 1993). On the writing of Spanish history, see Richard L. Kagan, "Clio and the Crown: Writing History in Habsburg Spain," in *Spain, Europe, and the Atlantic World: Essays in Honour of John H. Elliott*, ed. Richard L. Kagan and Geoffrey Parker (Cambridge: Cambridge University Press, 1995), 73–99.

2. Over the course of several decades, the historian and literary scholar Américo Castro provided the crucial critical re-evaluation of this mythical Spain, emphasizing the importance of medieval *convivencia* and tracing the Semitic origins of key early modern Spanish figures.

3. Etienne Balibar, "The Nation Form: History and Ideology," in Etienne Balibar and Immanuel Wallerstein, *Race, Nation, Class: Ambiguous Identities,* trans. Chris Turner (London: Verso, 1991), 86–106.

4. Ibid., 86.

5. Sebastián de Covarrubias, *Tesoro de la lengua castellana o española* (1611), ed. Martín de Riquer (1943; reprint, Barcelona: Alta Fulla, 1998), 823. Unless otherwise noted, all translations from the Spanish are mine.

6. On *limpieza,* see Henry Kamen, *Inquisition and Society in Spain in the Sixteenth and Seventeenth Centuries* (Bloomington: Indiana University Press, 1985); Julio Caro Baroja, *Los judíos en la España moderna y contemporánea,* 3 vols. (Madrid: Istmo, 1978); Albert Sicroff, *Los estatutos de limpieza de sangre: Controversias entre los siglos XV y XVII,* trans. Mauro Armiño (Madrid: Taurus, 1985); and Antonio Domínguez Ortiz, *Las clases privilegiadas en el Antiguo Régimen* (Madrid: Istmo, 1973). Domínguez Ortiz describes the obsession with pure blood as "la auténtica peculiaridad española" (14) (the real Spanish peculiarity). Kamen challenges what he considers the excessive emphasis on the statutes, especially in literary studies, in "*Limpieza* and the Ghost of Américo Castro: Racism as a Tool of Literary Analysis," *Hispanic Review* 64.1 (Winter 1996): 19–26.

7. For the increasing repression of the Moriscos, see Deborah Root, "Speaking Christian: Orthodoxy and Difference in Sixteenth-Century Spain," *Representations* 23 (Summer 1988): 118–134; Julio Caro Baroja, *Los moriscos del reino de Granada* (Madrid: Istmo, 1976); and Antonio Domínguez Ortiz and Bernard Vincent, *Historia de los moriscos: Vida y tragedia de una minoría* (Madrid: Revista de Occidente, 1978).

8. For the representation of Muslims and Jews as both nonmale and non-Spanish, see George Mariscal's fine reading of Huarte de San Juan and Juan de Timoneda in *Contradictory Subjects: Quevedo, Cervantes, and Seventeenth-Century Spanish Culture* (Ithaca, N.Y.: Cornell University Press, 1991), 57–61.

9. Josiah Blackmore and Gregory S. Hutcheson, Introduction to *Queer Iberia: Sexualities, Cultures, and Crossings from the Middle Ages to the Renaissance,* ed. Josiah Blackmore and Gregory S. Hutcheson (Durham, N.C.: Duke University Press, 1999), 12.

10. Claire Sponsler, *Drama and Resistance: Bodies, Goods, and Theatricality in Late Medieval England* (Minneapolis: University of Minnesota Press, 1997), 2.

11. Carmen Bernís notes that this early law, passed by the Catholic kings in 1499, created a distinction that disappeared by the reign of Charles V, by which time, in theory at least, nobles and burghers had the right to wear the same materials. See *Indumentaria española en tiempos de Carlos V* (Madrid: Consejo Superior de Investigaciones Científicas, 1962), 9.

12. Quoted in ibid., 14.

13. Covarrubias, *Tesoro de la lengua,* 1003.

14. Félix Lope de Vega Carpio, *El caballero de Olmedo* (1620; reprint, Madrid: Cátedra, 1993), ll. 1588–94.

15. For Moorish attire among Christians, see Carmen Bernís, "Modas moriscas en la sociedad cristiana española del siglo XV y principios del XVI," *Boletín de la Real Academia de la Historia* 144 (1959): 199–228; and Ruth Matilda Anderson, *Hispanic Costume, 1480–1530* (New York: Hispanic Society of America, 1979).

16. Bernís, "Modas moriscas," 202.

17. For a related argument on the the staging of Jews in medieval drama, see Robert L. A. Clark and Claire Sponsler, "Othered Bodies: Racial Cross-Dressing in the *Mistere de la Sainte Hostie* and the Croxton *Play of the Sacrament,*" *Journal of Medieval and Early Modern Studies* 29.1 (Winter 1999): 61–87.

18. On the so-called maurophilic literature of the late sixteenth century, see María Soledad Carrasco-Urgoiti, *The Moorish Novel: El "Abencerraje" and Pérez de Hita* (Boston: Twayne, 1976).

19. Miguel de Cervantes Saavedra, *El ingenioso hidalgo Don Quijote de la Mancha* (1605, 1615), ed. Martín de Riquer (Barcelona: Planeta, 1997), II.63, 65. Subsequent references to *Don Quijote* appear parenthetically in the text either by page number or by part and chapter number.

20. See, among others, Margo Hendricks and Patricia Parker, eds., *Women, "Race," and Writing in the Early Modern Period* (London: Routledge, 1994); Kim F. Hall, *Things of Darkness: Economies of Race and Gender in Early Modern England* (Ithaca, N.Y.: Cornell University Press, 1995); Sponsler, *Drama and Resistance;* Clark and Sponsler,

"Othered Bodies"; Robert L. A. Clark and Claire Sponsler, "Queer Play: The Cultural Work of Cross-dressing in Medieval Drama," *New Literary History* 28 (1997): 319–44; Stephen Orgel, *Impersonations* (Cambridge: Cambridge University Press, 1996); and Blackmore and Hutcheson, *Queer Iberia.*

21. Francesca T. Royster, "White-limed Walls: Whiteness and Gothic Extremism in Shakespeare's *Titus Andronicus,*" *Shakespeare Quarterly* 51.4 (Winter 2000): 432–55.

22. For "racial drift," see Douglas R. Cope, *The Limits of Racial Denomination: Plebeian Society in Colonial Mexico City, 1660–1720* (Madison: University of Wisconsin Press, 1994); Robert McCaa, "Calidad, Clase, and Marriage in Colonial Mexico: The Case of Parral, 1788–90," *Hispanic American Historical Review* 64.3 (1984): 477–501; and Elizabeth Anne Kuznesof, "Ethnic and Gender Influences on 'Spanish' Creole Society in Colonial Spanish America," *Colonial Latin American Review* 4.1 (1995): 153–76.

23. Kuznesof, "Ethnic and Gender Influences," 169. See also Stuart B. Schwartz's response to Kuznesof, "Colonial Identities and the *Sociedad de Castas,*" *Colonial Latin American Review* 4.1 (1995): 185–201.

24. Sherry Velasco, *The Lieutenant Nun: Transgenderism, Lesbian Desire, and Catalina de Erauso* (Austin: University of Texas Press, 2000).

25. Israel Burshatin, "Written on the Body: Slave or Hermaphrodite in Sixteenth-Century Spain," in *Queer Iberia,* ed. Blackmore and Hutcheson, 422, 436–41.

26. See Eric Lott, *Love and Theft: Blackface Minstrelsy and the American Working Class* (New York: Oxford University Press, 1993); and Michael Rogin, *Black Face, White Noise: Jewish Immigrants in the Hollywood Melting Pot* (Berkeley: University of California Press, 1996).

27. Rogin, *Black Face, White Noise,* 34.

28. Marjorie Garber, *Vested Interests: Cross-Dressing and Cultural Anxiety* (New York: Routledge, 1992), 16.

29. There is a large body of recent work on passing in the Harlem Renaissance. See, among others, Judith Butler, "Passing, Queering: Nella Larsen's Psychoanalytic Challenge," in *Female Subjects in Black and White: Race, Psychoanalysis, Feminism,* ed. Elizabeth Abel et al. (Berkeley: University of California Press, 1997), 266–84.

30. The indispensable account of Mediterranean geopolitics in the period is Fernand Braudel's *The Mediterranean and the Mediterranean World in the Age of Philip II,* 2 vols., trans. Siân Reynolds (London: Collins, 1973). In *The Forgotten Frontier: A History of the Sixteenth-Century Ibero-African Frontier* (Chicago: University of Chicago Press, 1978), Andrew C. Hess disputes Braudel's emphasis on the continuities and similarities among Mediterranean peoples, arguing instead that "the separation of the Mediterranean world into different, well-defined cultural spheres is the main theme of its sixteenth-century history" (3).

31. On renegades, see Bartolomé Bennassar and Lucile Bennassar, *Los cristianos de Alá: La fascinante aventura de los renegados,* trans. José Luis Gil Aristu (Madrid: Nerea, 1989). On captivity, see Ellen G. Friedman, *Spanish Captives in North Africa in the Early Modern Age* (Madison: University of Wisconsin Press, 1983).

32. See Jean Canavaggio, "À propos de deux *comedias* de Cervantès: Quelques re-

marques sur un manuscript récemment retrouvé," *Bulletin Hispanique* 63 (1966): 5–29.

33. See Ellen M. Anderson, "Playing at Moslem and Christian: The Construction of Gender and the Representation of Faith in Cervantes' Captivity Plays," *Cervantes* 13 (1993): 37–59.

34. For Cervantes's imaginative reworkings of orthodox ideologies, see E. Michael Gerli's reading of the Captive's tale in the first part of *Don Quijote* as a "deliverance from the racial hatred and intolerance that preside over the Spanish discourse of history and the foundational fiction of Reconquest" in *Refiguring Authority: Reading, Writing, and Rewriting in Cervantes* (Lexington: University Press of Kentucky, 1995), 54.

35. See Bennassar and Bennassar, *Los cristianos;* and Nabil Matar, *Turks, Moors, and Englishmen in the Age of Discovery* (New York: Columbia University Press, 1999).

36. "Relación de la gran presa que hizieron quatro Galeras de la Religión de San Iuan, de dos Naues, y seis Caramuçales, y dos Galeras Turquescas, con el número de Cautiuos, y Christianos libertados" (1617), in *Los turcos en el Mediterráneo: Relaciones,* ed. Ignacio Bauer Landauer (Madrid: Ed. Ibero-africano-americana, n.d.), 90–91.

37. Diego de Haedo, *Topografía e historia de Argel* (1612), 3 vols. (Madrid: Sociedad de Bibliófilos Españoles, 1927), 1:52–53.

38. Matar, *Turks, Moors, and Englishmen,* 51.

39. Both are quoted ibid., 51–52.

40. Hess, *Forgotten Frontier,* 42.

41. Bennassar and Bennassar, *Los cristianos,* 268.

42. Both of their stories are told in ibid., 292.

43. Amy Robinson, "It Takes One to Know One: Passing and Communities of Common Interest," *Critical Inquiry* 20 (Summer 1994): 715–36.

44. For markers of difference in medieval and early modern European theater, see Clark and Sponsler, "Othered Bodies."

45. See Friedman, *Spanish Captives,* 107–23. By the reign of Philip II, redemptions involved such large sums of money that the Spanish state began overseeing the work of the religious orders.

46. Ibid., 147.

47. Hess, *Forgotten Frontier,* 124. See also Peter Earle, *Corsairs of Malta and Barbary* (London: Sidgwick and Jackson, 1970).

48. See Bennassar and Bennassar, *Los cristianos,* especially the cases of Francesco Guicciardo and Guillaume Bedos and the section entitled "Revindicación de la identidad turca y de la fe musulmana" (482–89).

49. My argument on passing is analogous to Jonathan Goldberg's on sodomy. He notes that any inquiry into sodomy "will never deliver the sodomite per se, but only . . . sodometries, relational structures precariously available to prevailing discourses" (*Sodometries: Renaissance Texts, Modern Sexualities* [Stanford, Calif.: Stanford University Press, 1992], 20).

50. Clark and Sponsler, "Othered Bodies," 65.

51. Domínguez Ortiz, *Las clases privilegiadas*, 21; and Sicroff, *Los estatutos*, 160 and passim.

52. On Cervantes's rewriting of both literary traditions and specific texts, see Gerli, *Refiguring Authority.*

53. For a survey of the critical views of Cervantes's "development" from idealism to realism, or vice versa, see Ruth S. El Saffar, *Novel to Romance: A Study of Cervantes's "Novelas ejemplares"* (Baltimore: Johns Hopkins University Press, 1974), 169–77.

54. Ibid., 21, 29.

55. On the play of realism and romance, see, among others, Edwin Williamson, *The Halfway House of Fiction: Don Quixote and Arthurian Romance* (Oxford: Oxford University Press, 1984); and Gerli, *Refiguring Authority.*

56. Miguel de Cervantes Saavedra, *Los trabajos de Persiles y Sigismunda* (1617), ed. Juan Bautista Avalle-Arce (Madrid: Clásicos Castalia, 1969), 284. The English translations come from Celia Richmond Weller and Clark A. Colahan's *The Trials of Persiles and Sigismunda: A Northern Story* (Berkeley: University of California Press, 1989), 200. My changes to their translations appear in brackets.

57. Lope wrote the "Arte Nuevo" in 1609 as a speech to be read at the Madrid Academy. I quote from the text published in Emilio Orozco Díaz, *¿Qué es el "Arte nuevo" de Lope de Vega?* (Salamanca: Universidad de Salamanca, 1978), 70.

58. For an eleven-page list of Golden Age stage works that involved female-to-male cross-dressing, see Carmen Bravo-Villasante, *La mujer vestida de hombre en el teatro español, siglos XVI–XVII* (Madrid: Revista de Occidente, 1955).

59. Ursula K. Heise, "Transvestism and the Stage Controversy in Spain and England, 1580–1680," *Theatre Journal* 44 (1992): 357–74, quote on 358.

60. For a reading of *El vergonzoso en palacio* as a thematization of "the universal appeal of the transvestite," see ibid., 372–74.

61. For a reading that stresses the interconnection between gender and ethnicity in Cervantes's *comedias de cautivos,* see Anderson, "Playing at Moslem and Christian."

Chapter 2: Border Crossings

1. Michel Foucault, *The Order of Things: An Archaeology of the Human Sciences* (New York: Pantheon, 1973), 47.

2. For romance cross-dressing, see Winfried Schleiner, "Male Cross-Dressing and Transvestism in Renaissance Romances," *Sixteenth Century Journal* 19 (Spring 1988): 605–19. For the martial maid tradition, see Carol Ruprecht, "The Martial Maid: Androgyny in Epic from Virgil to the Poets of the Italian Renaissance" (Ph.D. diss., Yale University, 1977); Valeria Finucci, *The Lady Vanishes: Subjectivity and Representation in Castiglione and Ariosto* (Stanford, Calif.: Stanford University Press, 1992), 227–54; and Elizabeth J. Bellamy, *Translations of Power: Narcissism and the Unconscious in Epic History* (Ithaca, N.Y.: Cornell University Press, 1992). Bravo-Villasante gives an overview of both traditions in *La mujer vestida de hombre,* 33–58. Velasco discusses both historical and theatrical instances of warrior women in *Lieutenant Nun,* 31–35.

3. See Heise, "Transvestism and the Stage Controversy"; and Stephen Orgel, "Nobody's Perfect; or, Why Did the English Stage Take Boys for Women?" *South Atlantic Quarterly* 88 (Winter 1989): 7–28.

4. Heise, "Transvestism and the Stage Controversy," 358; and Velasco, *Lieutenant Nun*, 35–43.

5. Finucci quotes Freud's "Femininity" to convey a sense of this confusion: "'When you meet a human being, the first distinction you make is "male or female?" and you are accustomed to make the distinction with unhesitating certainty'" (*Lady Vanishes*, 199).

6. For masculine women, see Sherry Velasco, "Marimachos, hombrunas, barbudas: The Masculine Woman in Cervantes," *Cervantes* 20.1 (Spring 2000): 69–78; and Mary S. Gossy, "Aldonza as Butch: Narrative and the Play of Gender in *Don Quijote*," in *¿Entiendes?: Queer Readings, Hispanic Writings*, ed. Emilie L. Bergmann and Paul Julian Smith (Durham, N.C.: Duke University Press, 1995), 17–28.

7. Jacobo Sanz Hermida notes the role of beards as central gender markers in "Aspectos fisiológicos de la Dueña Dolorida: La metamorfosis de la mujer en hombre," in *Actas del Tercer Coloquio Internacional de la Asociación de Cervantistas, Alcalá de Henares, 12–16 Nov. 1990* (Barcelona: Anthropos, 1993), 463–72.

8. Butler, *Gender Trouble*, 141.

9. In "Cervantes, Goytisolo, and the Sodomitical Scene" (in *Cervantes and the Modernists: The Question of Influence*, ed. Edwin Williamson [London: Támesis, 1994]), Paul Julian Smith argues that, despite the recognition of Dorotea's femaleness, the scene "summons up the spectacle of homosexual affect in a moment of hesitation" (46).

10. Ambroise Paré recounts similar stories of white babies born to black parents or black babies born to white parents in "Exemples de monstres qui se font par imagination," in *Des Monstres et Prodiges* (1573; reprint, Geneva: Droz, 1971), 35–37.

11. David Quint, *Epic and Empire: Politics and Generic Form from Virgil to Milton* (Princeton, N.J.: Princeton University Press, 1993), 234–37.

12. Butler, *Gender Trouble*, 141.

13. Butler bases her definition of "camp" on this sense of a parodic recontextualization of the "construction of the illusion of a primary and interior gendered self" (ibid., 138).

14. Velasco, "Marimachos, hombrunas, barbudas," 72–73.

15. Finucci, *Lady Vanishes*, 237 and passim.

16. Quint, *Epic and Empire*, 234–47.

17. See Riquer's extensive editorial note (1000–1001) on the *bandolers* in *Don Quijote*, II.60. In "Bearded Waiting Women, Lovely Lethal Piratemen: Sexual Boundary Shifts in *Don Quijote*, Part II" (*Cervantes* 2 [1983]: 155–64), Arthur Efron connects crossdressing with "the increased exploration, in the last part of the novel, of social authority" (162).

18. Notice that the other, much more developed instance of a dying lover in *Don Quijote* is the case of Marcela and Grisóstomo, where the woman occupies a similarly "masculine" position of liberty and independence. And in that case also, despite Mar-

cela's impassioned denials, the "masculine" woman cannot quite shake off the accusations of murder.

19. Ricote's exchange with his old neighbor Sancho alternately supports and complicates certain features of Ana's story. Sancho confirms Ana's account of her immense sorrow at leaving Spain; Ricote, meanwhile, describes the many assimilated Moriscos who make their way back to Spain but adamantly affirms that his daughter was never informed of the whereabouts of his own treasure, which he has come to recover. He also refers to her as "Ricota" instead of by the name she later gives herself and to Ana's lover as Pedro instead of Gaspar Gregorio. The ambiguity of the names underscores the thematics of passing in these episodes: Ana Félix and Gaspar Gregorio seem to be claiming the ability to refashion their own identities as they see fit—in her case, by moving beyond genealogical determinism; in his, by eluding the obligations associated with his name and the shame of consorting with a Morisca.

20. On the anxieties surrounding interfaith unions and the penetration of the Spanish language by Arabic, see Benjamin Liu, "'Affined to love the Moor': Sexual Misalliance and Cultural Mixing in the *Cantigas d'escarnho e de mal dizer*," in *Queer Iberia*, ed. Blackmore and Hutcheson, 48–72.

21. On the androgyne as Cervantes's figure for "a kind of mutual, or nondominant, sexual difference that would displace hierarchy," see Diana de Armas Wilson, *Allegories of Love: Cervantes' "Persiles and Sigismunda"* (Princeton, N.J.: Princeton University Press, 1991), 78–105, quote on 79. By contrast, Carroll B. Johnson, in "La sexualidad en el *Quijote*" (*Edad de Oro* 9 [1990]: 125–36), reads the "neutralization" of the sexual difference between Ana and Don Gregorio as a signal of "la esterilidad de la política racial-étnica del gobierno de Felipe III" (135) (the sterility of the ethnoracial policy of Philip III's regime).

22. Orgel, "Nobody's Perfect," 20.

23. Heise, "Transvestism and the Stage Controversy," 364, 365. On the persecution of sodomy in Spain, see William Monter, *Frontiers of Heresy: The Spanish Inquisition from the Basque Lands to Sicily* (Cambridge: Cambridge University Press, 1990); Rafael Carrasco, *Inquisición y represión sexual en Valencia: Historia de los sodomitas, 1565–1785* (Barcelona: Laertes, 1985); and Mary Elizabeth Perry, "The 'Nefarious Sin' in Early Modern Seville," in *The Pursuit of Sodomy: Male Homosexuality in Renaissance and Enlightenment Europe*, ed. Kent Gerard and Gert Hekma (New York: Harrington Park Press, 1989), 67–89.

24. On sodomy among the Moors, see Diego de Haedo, *Topografía*, 1:176–77. For modern critical accounts of this prejudice, see Matar, *Turks, Moors, and Englishmen*, 109–27; and Paul Julian Smith, "'The Captive's Tale': Race, Text, Gender," in *Quixotic Desire: Psychoanalytic Perspectives on Cervantes*, ed. Ruth Anthony El Saffar and Diana de Armas Wilson (Ithaca, N.Y.: Cornell University Press, 1993), 227–38. For further studies on homoeroticism within the world of Islam, see *Homoeroticism in Classical Arabic Literature*, ed. J. W. Wright Jr. and Everett K. Rowson (New York: Columbia University Press, 1997); and *Islamic Homosexualities: Culture, History, and Literature*, ed. Stephen O. Murray and Will Roscoe (New York: New York University Press, 1997).

25. Note the relationship between captivity and sodomy in the first Captive's tale (in part I), in which the Spanish captive introduces the Venetian renegade Azán Agá as follows: "siendo grumete de una nave, le cautivó el Uchalí, y le quiso tanto, que fue uno de los más regalados garzones suyos" (426) (while he was a cabin boy, he was captured by Uchalí, who was so fond of him that he became one of his most pampered catamites).

26. For a discussion of the ambiguity of renegades, see Smith, "'Captive's Tale.'"

27. Heise, "Transvestism and the Stage Controversy," 364.

28. Ibid., 369.

29. In "Romance and Realism in the *Quixote*" (*Cervantes* 2 [1982]: 43–67), Edwin Williamson suggests that Ana's story "is unfinished because it cannot be concluded within the terms of the literary tradition from which it springs. . . . What stands between [Ana and Gregorio] is an inescapable historical reality—Philip III's edict expelling the Moriscos from Spain in 1609" (63–64).

Chapter 3: Empire Unmanned

1. As Antonio Rey Hazas points out in *Cervantes: Seminario sobre el estado actual de los estudios cervantinos* (Madrid: Centro de Estudios Cervantinos, 1995), s.v. "*Novelas ejemplares*," there are no *dos doncellas*—in the sense of "maids"—in the story, for one of them admits that she has lost her virginity to Marco Antonio. From the start, then, the novella plays with the triteness of romance convention and encourages the reader to question its categories.

2. Miguel de Cervantes Saavedra, "Las dos doncellas," in *Novelas ejemplares*, 2 vols., ed. Harry Sieber (Madrid: Cátedra, 1990), 2:201. Subsequent references to the novellas are to this edition and appear parenthetically in the text and notes by volume and page number or by page number only (where the volume number is obvious).

3. Some of the novellas were written years before publication. The first part of *Don Quijote* refers to one of them, "Novela de Rinconete y Cortadillo" (I.47). This novella appears with "El celoso extremeño" in a 1606 manuscript. For the critical debate on the chronology of the remaining novellas, see Rey Hazas, "*Novelas ejemplares*," 179–84.

4. For the general critical predisposition against romance in Cervantes, see El Saffar, *Novel to Romance*.

5. For my account of romance, I rely primarily on Patricia Parker, *Inescapable Romance: Studies in the Poetics of a Mode* (Princeton, N.J.: Princeton University Press, 1979). Fredric Jameson's "Magical Narratives: On the Dialectical Use of Genre Criticism" (in *The Political Unconscious* [Ithaca, N.Y.: Cornell University Press, 1981], 103–50) is another essential point of reference but focuses on the medieval tradition to the exclusion of the Renaissance romance.

6. For an indispensable account of the connection between epic and the ideology of empire, as well as the concomitant role of romance, see Quint, *Epic and Empire*. For romance's error with respect to epic, see Parker, *Inescapable Romance*.

7. See Tanner, *Last Descendant of Aeneas*, 141–43.

8. Jameson, "Magical Narratives," 105.

9. Anthony J. Cascardi, *Ideologies of History in the Spanish Golden Age* (University Park: Penn State University Press, 1997), 321.

10. The (s)wordplay is untranslatable.

11. For the history of banditry in Catalonia, see Ricardo García Cárcel, *Historia de Cataluña, siglos XVI–XVII: Los caracteres originales de la historia de Cataluña* (Barcelona: Ariel, 1985), 245–62; and J. H. Elliott, *The Revolt of the Catalans: A Study in the Decline of Spain, 1598–1640* (Cambridge: Cambridge University Press, 1963), 51–52 and passim.

12. Elliott, *Revolt of the Catalans*, 110.

13. In an interesting echo of "Las dos doncellas," Roque Guinart spares both soldiers on the way to Naples and noble pilgrims, taking from them only a token sum of money. On Cervantes's recuperation of the marginalized bandit and the representation of Roque Guinart as an example of "distributive justice," see Enrique Martínez López, "Sobre la amnistía de Roque Guinart: El laberinto de la *bandositat* catalana y los moriscos en el *Quijote*," *Cervantes* 11 (1991): 69–85.

14. In *Inquisition and Society in Spain in the Sixteenth and Seventeenth Centuries* (Bloomington: Indiana University Press, 1985), Henry Kamen points out that Jews led a "comparatively tranquil existence" in Italy, where the Spanish concern with blood purity was often scorned (256).

15. Joaquín Casalduero notes the curious similarities between Leocadia's story of uncertain paternity and the tale of the cross-dressing "daughter of Diego de la Llana" in *Don Quijote* (II.49), which I discuss in chapter 2, in *Sentido y forma de las "Novelas ejemplares"* (Madrid: Gredos, 1969), 206.

16. According to Covarrubias, *adorno* may refer also to rhetorical enrichments— "figuras y colores retóricos" (*Tesoro de la lengua*, 41). Is Cervantes here alluding to the rich polysemy of his own text?

17. See Ruth Pike, *Enterprise and Adventure: The Genoese in Seville and the Opening of the New World* (Ithaca, N.Y.: Cornell University Press, 1966); and Braudel, *Mediterranean and the Mediterranean World*, 1:501.

18. Braudel, *Mediterranean and the Mediterranean World*, 1:394.

19. Ibid., 1:393. See also J. H. Elliott, "The Decline of Spain," in *Crisis in Europe, 1560–1660: Essays from "Past and Present,"* ed. Trevor Aston (London: Routledge, 1965), 167–93. For a detailed description of *asientos, juros,* and other types of borrowing, see Felipe Ruiz Martín, "Las finanzas españolas durante el reinado de Felipe II," *Hispania: Cuadernos de historia* (1968): 109–73; and Geoffrey Parker, *The Army of Flanders and the Spanish Road, 1567–1659* (Cambridge: Cambridge University Press, 1972), 145–56.

20. Quevedo, "Poderoso caballero es Don Dinero," in *Poesía varia*, ed. James O. Crosby (Madrid: Cátedra, 1981), 9–12.

21. Braudel, *Mediterranean and the Mediterranean World*, 1:490–93; and Elliott, *Revolt of the Catalans*, 110.

22. Elliott describes a notorious incident near Igualada in 1612, when 16,000 *escu-*

dos belonging to "the Genoese and other private persons" were stolen from a convoy, and an even more spectacular heist in 1613, when 108 cases of silver being sent to Italy for the king's service by one of his Genoese bankers were looted by more than a hundred bandits, with some help from the locals (*Revolt of the Catalans*, 110–11). Although sizable robberies had occurred as early as the 1580s, the Crown continued to use the Catalonian route to Italy.

23. On the marriages between Genoese and noble Spanish families, see Pike, *Enterprise and Adventure*, 3–8.

24. Quoted in Ruth Pike, "The Image of the Genoese in Golden Age Literature," *Hispania* 46 (1963): 705–14, quote on 705 (my translation).

25. Elliott, *Revolt of the Catalans*, 44.

26. Although there is a long-standing critical fascination with Cervantes's praise for Barcelona, including Juan Suñé Benages's *Elogios de Cervantes a Barcelona* and Manuel de Montoliú and José María Casas's *Cervantes y sus elogios a Barcelona*, first published in *Boletín de la Real Academia de Buenas Letras de Barcelona* 12 (1925–26): 463–560 and 13 (1927–28): 35–140, respectively, very little has been written about the turmoil that so abruptly follows Cervantes's praise. In *Cervantes en Barcelona* (Barcelona: Sirmio, 1989), Martín de Riquer is concerned mostly with establishing the likelihood of Cervantes's sojourn in the city in the summer of 1610. He recounts one violent incident between upper-class revelers and galley slaves as a possible model for the battle in "Las dos doncellas" but admits that "the real episode and the one in the novella are somewhat different" (87–88). In "Las dos doncellas," the battle seems to involve the whole city, until the noble Sancho de Cardona restrains the populace.

27. *Dietari de Jeroni Pujades*, vol. 1: *1601–1605*, ed. Josep M. Casas Homs (Barcelona: Fundació Casajuana, 1975), 221 (entry for Dec. 1, 1602).

28. On the general population decline in Spain at the turn of the seventeenth century due to emigration, military service, and plague, see Elliott, "Decline of Spain," 174–77.

29. For an account of Moorish raids and the Barcelona galleys' defense of the coast, see Riquer, *Cervantes en Barcelona*, 47–50.

30. The first royal order of expulsion, for Valencia, was signed in August 1609; the one for Catalonia, in April 1610. For a precise chronology of the expulsions and for Pujades's reaction, see ibid., 57.

31. In this context, Marco Antonio Adorno's more specific destination in Naples may also be significant. As Antonio Calabria points out in *The Cost of Empire: The Finances of the Kingdom of Naples in the Time of Spanish Rule* (Cambridge: Cambridge University Press, 1991), Genoese bankers "acquired a stranglehold on finances in Naples, as in Castile, and they added profit to profiteering as they dominated the shipping industry, the export trade, the provisioning of the city of Naples and the fiscal machinery of the state" (5). In 1609, Philip III granted Genoese bankers the right to send their own agents to Naples to levy direct taxes to repay themselves for loans to the Crown.

32. As Carroll B. Johnson notes, the historical Sancho de Cardona, admiral of Aragon, was a progressive aristocrat whose pronounced religious tolerance for the Moris-

cos eventually led to his conviction by the Inquisition in 1569 (*Cervantes and the Material World* [Urbana: University of Illinois Press, 2000], 60). It is striking that the supremely benevolent figure in "Las dos doncellas," who knits together the disparate Spaniards with his courtesy, should be precisely a protector of New Christians.

33. Félix Lope de Vega Carpio, *El desconfiado*, in *Obras de Lope de Vega*, vol. 4 (Madrid: Real Academia Española, 1917), 500.

34. Tirso de Molina, *En Madrid y en una casa*, in *Obras dramáticas completas*, 3 vols., ed. Blanca de los Ríos (Madrid: Aguilar, 1958), 3:1256–57.

35. Elsewhere, Cervantes pokes fun at the romance convention of ignoring such material concerns. When Don Quijote first becomes a knight (I.3), the innkeeper informs him in no uncertain terms that he must carry money, despite the fact that it is not mentioned in the chivalric romances.

36. Virgil, *Aeneid*, 8.685. For an account of the central place of Actium and its imperial ideology in the *Aeneid* and the subsequent epic tradition, see Quint, *Epic and Empire*, 21–49. The story of Mark Antony was familiar to readers in early modern Spain not only from the epic tradition that Quint describes but also from Plutarch's *Lives*, which had been translated into Castilian by the late fifteenth century. In the burlesque prologue to part I of *Don Quijote*, the author's friend recommends Plutarch for stories of valiant captains: "Plutarco os dará mil Alejandros" (17). See also Aurelio Pérez Jiménez, "Plutarco y el humanismo español del renacimiento," in *Estudios sobre Plutarco: Obra y tradición—Actas del I symposion español sobre Plutarco*, ed. Aurelio Pérez Jiménez and Gonzalo del Cerro Calderón (Málaga: Delegación Provincial de Cultura, 1990), 229–47.

37. Cervantes pairs the names of the two betrayers again, in a more jocular vein, in the plaintive ballad that Altisidora, the duchess's lady-in-waiting, addresses to Don Quijote over his supposed theft of her stays (II.57). The refrain is repeated after every verse:

> Tú has burlado, monstruo horrendo,
> la más hermosa doncella
> que Diana vio en sus montes,
> que Venus miró en sus selvas.
> *Cruel Vireno, fugitivo Eneas,*
> *Barrabás te acompañe, allá te avengas.* (977–78)

> [You horrid monster, you have deceived the most beautiful damsel that Diana ever saw in her hills or Venus in her forests. Cruel Bireno, fleeing Aeneas: may Barrabas go with you, may evil befall you.]

The recycling of the pairing in this burlesque episode suggests that Cervantes may have deliberately disarmed his own mechanisms of allusion through farcical repetition.

38. As Harry Vélez Quiñones points out in "Angels and Pilgrims: Gender Instability and Its Containment in Cervantes' 'Las dos doncellas'" (paper presented at the Cervantes Society meeting, San Francisco, Dec. 1998), Leocadia returns dressed as a pilgrim despite Rafael's promise to bring her home wearing "vuestro propio, honra-

do y verdadero traje" ("Las dos doncellas," 232) (your own honest and true costume) if she agrees to marry him.

39. Cf. Cervantes's "La señora Cornelia," in which two young Spanish gentlemen abandon their studies at Salamanca (where Marco Antonio was also a student [208]) for Flanders: "llevados del hervor de la sangre moza y del deseo, como decirse suele, de ver mundo, y por parecerles que el ejercicio de las armas, aunque arma y dice bien a todos, principalmente asienta y dice mejor en los bien nacidos y de ilustre sangre" (241) (moved by the ebullience of young blood and the desire, as they say, to see the world, and because it seemed to them that the exercise of arms, although it arms and befits all men, principally suits and befits those well born and of illustrious blood). The latter rationale is immediately undercut as the two arrive in Flanders only to find that there is a truce on and nothing for them to do. They then decide to visit Italy before returning home and, captivated by Bologna, continue their studies there.

In "La gitanilla," Italy becomes a haven from the law, thanks to the financial connections I describe earlier. Having killed a man, Clemente escapes to Italy on Genoese galleys, on which "un caballero ginovés, grande amigo del Conde mi pariente . . . suele enviar a Génova gran cantidad de plata" (115) (a Genoese gentleman, a great friend of my relative the Count, often sends a large quantity of silver to Genoa).

40. See Monter, *Frontiers of Heresy*; Carrasco, *Inquisición y represión sexual*; and M. Herrero García, *Ideas de los españoles del siglo XVII* (Madrid: Voluntad, 1928).

41. Herrero García, *Ideas de los españoles*, 367; and Perry, "'Nefarious Sin,'" 82.

42. Herrero García quotes from Castillo Solórzano's *El comisario de figuras*, a satirical account of a pretty lad who has learned "Italian" ways:

> "Comisario: Mozo estáis, pues en vos cana no asoma, y ha mucho que pasó lo de Sodoma. ¿Enrizáis el cabello?
> Lindo: Y con algalia.
> Comisario: Este huevo ha pasado por Italia." (*Ideas de los españoles*, 367)
>
> [Commissary: You are young, for you have no gray hairs, and that Sodom affair was long ago. Do you curl your hair?
> Dandy: And with civet.
> Commissary: This egg has passed through Italy.]

43. *Dietaria Pujades* (1:293), quoted in Monter, *Frontiers of Heresy*, 291–92 (my translation). Monter notes that in Italy, conversely, Spaniards were particularly vulnerable to prosecution for sodomy.

Chapter 4: Passing Pleasures

1. Critics have often noted the Byzantine qualities of the novella. See, for example, Juan Bautista Avalle-Arce's introduction to his edition of the *Novelas ejemplares*, 3 vols. (Madrid: Castalia, 1982), in which he comments that the similarities to Heliodorus or Achilles Tatius are qualified by the novella's focus on Sicily—part of Spain's empire—and on the historically accurate scourge of piracy (1:30). Ruth El Saffar argues that

"Cervantes protects the story's credibility by making even the most unlikely episodes appear at least possible and by placing his fictional characters in a well-known historical situation" (*Novel to Romance*, 139).

2. As William Clamurro suggests in "'El amante liberal' de Cervantes y las fronteras de la identidad" (*AIH Actas* 5 [1992]: 193–200), "esta ubicación en un momento histórico y lugares culturalmente intermedios y fronterizos produce un rico trasfondo alusivo que realza el problema de la identidad, tanto personal . . . como colectiva" (193) (This location in a historical moment and in culturally intermediate and border spaces produces a rich background of allusion that highlights the problem of identity, both personal . . . and collective). Clamurro focuses on the symbolic connections that enable developments in the characters' identities.

3. Andreas Mahler, "Italian Vices: Cross-cultural Constructions of Temptation and Desire in English Renaissance Drama," in *Shakespeare's Italy: Functions of Italian Locations in Renaissance Drama*, ed. Michele Marrapodi, A. J. Henselaars, Marcello Capuzzo, and L. Falzon Stantucci (Manchester: Manchester University Press, 1993), 51. See also "Italians and Others: Venice and the Irish in *Coryat's Crudities* and *The White Devil*" (*Renaissance Drama* 18 [1987]: 101–19), in which Ann Rosalind Jones suggests that Renaissance England constructed Italy "through a lens of voyeuristic curiosity through which writers and their audiences explored what was forbidden in their own culture" (101).

4. For the Spanish Empire in Sicily, see H. G. Koenigsberger, *The Practice of Empire* (emended ed. of *The Government of Sicily under Philip II of Spain*) (Ithaca, N.Y.: Cornell University Press, 1969).

5. Ibid., 45.

6. See Paul Julian Smith, "Cervantes, Goytisolo, and the Sodomitical Scene," in *Cervantes and the Modernists: The Question of Influence*, ed. Edwin Williamson (London: Támesis, 1994), 43–54; Clamurro, "'El amante liberal'"; and Miguel Angel Vázquez, "Mahamut, el buen salvaje: Nacionalismo y maurofilia en 'El amante liberal' de Cervantes," *Romance Languages Annual* 7 (1995): 642–46.

7. Edwin Williamson, "Hacia la conciencia ideológica de Cervantes: Idealización y violencia en 'El amante liberal,'" in *Cervantes: Estudios en la víspera de su centenario* (Keissel: Reichenberger, 1994), 527.

8. Johnson, *Cervantes and the Material World*, 133.

9. For the fall of Cyprus and its connection to the internecine war against the Moriscos in the Alpujarras, see Braudel, *Mediterranean and the Mediterranean World*, 2:1082–87.

10. Note the change of hypothetical subject from plural to singular in this long phrase. The sorrow seems to become more personal in the very telling of the city's fall.

11. On these historical figures see Johnson, *Cervantes and the Material World*, 120–23.

12. It is striking that the reader is never offered any mitigating circumstances for Mahamut's apostasy, any proof of his Christian sincerity, or even a Christian name for him. He refers vaguely to his "poca edad y menos entendimiento" (139) (scarce years

and even scarcer understanding) when he abandoned Christianity, but the text suggests he was not forced to convert as a child, for he recognizes the adult Leonisa from Ricardo's trite description of a local Petrarchan beauty (142).

13. On the very close connections between Christian and Muslim Greeks in the period, often within the same family, see Bennassar and Bennassar, *Los cristianos,* 214–28.

14. On the Inquisition's attitude toward renegades in Spain, see Bartolomé Bennassar, "Renégats et Inquisiteurs, XVIe–XVIIe siècles," in *Les problèmes de l'exclusion en Espagne, XVIe–XVIIe siècles: Idéologie et discours,* ed. Augustin Redondo (Paris: Sorbonne, 1983), 105–11. In *Los cristianos,* Bennassar and Bennassar point out that the Sicilian Inquisition seems to have been fairly lax with former female slaves eager to return to Christianity (333–34).

15. For uncertainties about the authenticity of renegades and captives, see Smith, "'Captive's Tale'"; E. Michael Gerli, "Rewriting Myth and History," in *Refiguring Authority,* 40–60; and the chapter "Pirating Spain" in Barbara Fuchs, *Mimesis and Empire: The New World, Islam, and European Identities* (Cambridge: Cambridge University Press, 2001), 139–63.

16. See, for example, Francisco Márquez Villanueva, "Leandra, Zoraida y sus fuentes franco-italianas," in *Personajes y temas del Quijote* (Madrid: Taurus, 1975), 77–146.

17. Gerli reads the Captive's tale as an "appeal for cultural and religious tolerance" in the face of Spanish historical reality (*Refiguring Authority,* 42).

18. On the eroticization of *moras* and the "borderotics" of Spain's fascination with Islam in the ballad tradition, see Louise O. Vasvári, *The Heterotextual Body of the "Mora Morilla,"* in *Papers of the Hispanic Research Seminar* (No. 12) (London: Queen Mary and Westfield College, 1999), 32–57.

19. Cf. "El licenciado Vidriera," in which Tomás satirizes conventional Petrarchism and its reliance on precious objects for its metaphors:

> Otra vez le preguntaron qué era la causa de que los poetas, por la mayor parte, eran pobres. Respondió que porque ellos querían, pues estaba en su mano ser ricos, si se sabían aprovechar de la ocasión que por momentos traían entre las manos, que eran las de sus damas, que todas eran riquísimas en extremo, pues tenían los cabellos de oro, frente de plata bruñida, los ojos de verdes esmeraldas, los dientes de marfil, los labios de coral y la garganta de cristal transparente, y lo que lloraban eran líquidas perlas. (60)

> [Another time he was asked why poets were, for the most part, poor. He answered that it was because they wanted to be, as prosperity was within their reach if they only took advantage of the opportunity within their grasp, for their ladies were most rich, with hair of gold, brows of bright silver, eyes of green emeralds, ivory teeth, coral lips, and throats of transparent crystal, and what they cried were liquid pearls.]

20. In the second part of *Guerras civiles de Granada* (1619) (ed. Paula Blanchard-Demouge [Madrid: Bailly-Baillière, 1913]), which recounts the fighting in the Alpujarras, Ginés Pérez de Hita describes another beautiful blonde Moor, Maleha, who is loved

by the hero, Tuzani. After the fall of Galera, Tuzani finds Maleha "tendida en el suelo, con aquella camisa labrada y los cabellos rubios como hebras de oro tendidos alrededor de su cuello, no parecía sino un bellísimo ángel" (II.331) (lying on the ground, with that embroidered shirt and her blonde locks like golden threads lying about her neck, resembling nothing so much as a beautiful angel). The Petrarchan description, which whitens Maleha, clearly evokes sympathy for the vanquished other.

21. In the context of a very different reading, Williamson argues that Cervantes introduces the Moor to show that "la belleza es un valor ideal que se muestra capaz de trascender hasta las más agudas divisiones y oposiciones de la realidad histórica, como es la de los cristianos y los turcos" ("Hacia la conciencia ideológica," 527) (beauty is an ideal value that shows itself capable of transcending even the sharpest divisions and oppositions of historical reality, such as those between Christians and Turks).

22. Mahamut's warning recalls Calisto's famous claim of adoration for Melibea, "Melibeo soy," in *La Celestina.*

23. The erotic was an important aspect of "maurophilia" in the period. Notable examples include the hugely popular novella *El Abencerraje* (1561), the story of Ozmín and Daraja interpolated in Mateo Alemán's *Guzmán de Alfarache* (1599), and Pérez de Hita's own story of Tuzani and Maleha. See Carrasco-Urgoiti, *Moorish Novel.*

24. Williamson suggests that the complementarity of the two poets is an example of a "dualidad *positiva*" (*positive* duality) and compares their poem to Anselmo and Clemente's shared song in "La gitanilla" ("Hacia la conciencia ideológica," 526).

25. Andalucía officially became part of Castille in 1492 with the fall of Granada. Catalonia was, of course, the most important territory of the Crown of Aragon.

26. Cervantes repeats these lines, verbatim, in *Los baños de Argel* (III: ll. 2144–53). It would be interesting to trace the implications of the erotic defeat in that much more jingoistic text.

27. On Charles V's conquest of Tunis and its subsequent reconquest by the Turks, see Hess, *Forgotten Frontier,* 75–76 and 94–95.

28. Smith, "Cervantes, Goytisolo," 47.

29. Williamson, "Hacia la conciencia ideológica," 528.

30. Note how different matters are in the Captive's tale, where the distinctive garb of a Christian captive is both valuable and scarce. Ruy Pérez de Viedma specifically notes that it was decided the renegade who accompanied them should dress as a captive in order not to alarm the inhabitants any further or call attention to themselves: "—acordamos que el renegado se desnudase las ropas del turco y se vistiese un gilecuelo o casaca de cautivo que uno de nosotros le dio luego, aunque se quedó en camisa" (I.41) ("we decided that the renegade should take off his Turk's attire and wear instead a captive's jacket that one of us quickly gave him, even though it stripped him to his shirt").

31. Smith, "Cervantes, Goytisolo," 49.

32. For a reading of Cornelio in light of classical and early modern topoi of effeminacy, see Adrienne L. Martín, "Rereading 'El amante liberal' in the Age of Contrapuntal Sexualities," in *Cervantes and His Postmodern Constituencies,* ed. Anne J. Cruz and Carroll B. Johnson (New York: Garland, 1998), 151–69.

33. For the dynamics of the bower of bliss in *Orlando Furioso* and *Gerusalemme liberata,* see A. Bartlett Giamatti, *The Earthly Paradise and the Renaissance Epic* (Princeton, N.J.: Princeton University Press, 1966), 137–64 and 179–210. For narrative and visual traditions of the emasculated hero in a woman's power, see Patricia Parker, *Literary Fat Ladies: Rhetoric, Gender, Property* (London: Methuen, 1987), 54–66.

34. For a full account of this association, see Quint, *Epic and Empire,* 21–46.

35. Smith calls the equation of Muslims and sodomites an observation "unvoiced but pervasive in 'El amante liberal'" and cites Sieber's rather odd note on the *cadí*'s ruling on sodomy as evidence ("Cervantes, Goytisolo," 49; the note reference is to Sieber's edition of *Novelas ejemplares,* 2:139n). My sense is that it is precisely the studious avoidance of explicit connections between Islam and sodomy in the novella that makes it so interesting. Although Mahamut claims power over his master (154), it is not clear where his power resides; and the only mention of beautiful captive boys is voiced by Ricardo, as he explains how his captor gives for Leonisa "seis cristianos, los cuatro para el remo, y dos muchachos hermosísimos, de nación corsos, y a mí con ellos" (149) (six Christians, four for the galleys, and two most beautiful boys, from Corsica, and me with them). The Turks are all passionate lovers of women and hugely jealous. However, they allow Christian captives access to their women because of their perceived emasculation: "quizá debe de ser que por ser cautivos no los tienen por hombres cabales" (166) (it may be that, as they are captives, they are not considered real men).

36. Recall Diego de Haedo's distinction between "Turks by nature" and "Turks by profession" (*Topografía,* 1:51–52): "llámanse turcos de naturaleza los que han venido o sus padres de Turquía" (we call Turks by nature those who come from Turkey or whose parents come from Turkey); while "los turcos de profesión son todos los renegados que siendo de sangre y padres cristianos, de su libre voluntad se hicieron turcos, renegando impíamente y despreciando a su Dios y Criador" (Turks by profession are all those renegades of Christian blood and born to Christian parents who became Turks of their own free will, impiously reneging and scorning their God and Creator). Haedo suggests that renegades are too cowardly to face the labors of slavery without converting and, moreover, that they are attracted to the sodomitic vices of the Turks (1:53).

37. Casalduero notices this set of equivalences but emphasizes the contrast between Turks and Christians: "Este fondo turco es un elemento decorativo, que, al mismo tiempo que da el volumen del viaje—el Cadí es una especie de obispo; el Bajá es como un virrey; la Puerta del Gran Señor es como decir la corte; el Visir-bajá y los cuatro bajaes, que forman el Gran Consejo del Turco, igual al Presidente y los oidores del Real Consejo, lo sumario de la justicia, la manera de proveer estos cargos y de tomar la residencia a los oficiales, el cambio de éstos, las costumbres de las mujeres turcas, son otros tantos trazos informativos, que al contrastar con las costumbres de España pintan la emoción del viaje y decoran con su exoticismo la narración—, permite, tratándose de los turcos, presentar una moral cómicamente inferior a la cristiana" (*Sentido y forma de las "Novelas ejemplares,"* 79) (This Turkish background is a decorative element that, even as it conveys the tenor of the voyage—the Cadí is a kind of bishop; the Pasha is

like a viceroy; the Porte of the Great Turk is like the court; the Vizier-Pasha and the four pashas who form the Great Counsel of the Turk are like the President and judges of the Royal Council; the speed of justice, the manner of granting offices and of evaluating officials, the change in these, the habits of Turkish women, are a series of informational sketches that, by contrasting with Spanish customs, convey the excitement of the journey and adorn the narration with exotic touches—this allows, in the case of the Turks, for the presentation of morals that are comically inferior to the Christian ones).

38. Johnson notes the possible hidden critique of Spain and points out the structural equivalences between Spain and the various locations of the novella: "Cyprus is to Constantinople as Sicily is to Madrid, an outlying province, in both cases also incidentally an island, governed by a viceroy-pasha on behalf of an absent sovereign" (*Cervantes and the Material World*, 120).

39. One fascinating possible model for this kind of censure is the Inca Garcilaso de la Vega's *Comentarios reales de los Incas* (1609), which disguises a critique of Spanish rapacity as a condemnation of Inca imperialism. For a brilliant discussion of this dynamic, see Margarita Zamora, *Language, Authority, and Indigenous History in the "Comentarios reales de los incas"* (Cambridge: Cambridge University Press, 1988).

40. On critics of the Spanish *residencia*, see Johnson, *Cervantes and the Material World*, 124.

41. It could be argued that the speaker himself further complicates matters. As a reluctant renegade, Mahamut's loyalties are somewhat dubious: does he begin criticizing the Turks simply for Ricardo's benefit?

42. For the chaotic nature of the Spanish judicial system in Sicily, see Koenigsberger, *Practice of Empire*, 90–93.

43. For the ironic representation of justice in "La gitanilla," see Gerli, *Refiguring Authority*, 24–39.

44. In the context of a novella that features the buying and selling of captives, as well as a critique of posts bought and sold, it is striking to recall Sancho's amazing project of upward mobility in *Don Quijote* (I.29), discussed in chapter 2. Sancho imagines selling Princess Micomicona's African subjects as the first step in acquiring a profitable sinecure: "—¿Qué se me da a mí que mis vasallos sean negros? ¿Habrá más que cargar con ellos y traerlos a España, donde los podré vender, y adonde me los pagarán de contado, de cuyo dinero podré comprar algún título o algún oficio con que vivir descansado todos los días de mi vida?" (314) ("What do I care if my vassals are black? Need I do more than load them up and bring them to Spain, where I can sell them for cash, with which I will buy some title or post that will allow me to live in ease for the rest of my life?").

45. On the importance of *mestizaje* and hybridity in *La gran sultana*, see George Mariscal, "*La gran sultana* and the Issue of Cervantes's Modernity," *Revista de estudios hispánicos* 28.2 (May 1994): 185–212; and Ellen M. Anderson, "Playing at Moslem and Christian: The Construction of Gender and the Representation of Faith in Cervantes' Captivity Plays," *Cervantes* 13 (1993): 37–59.

46. Jean Canavaggio, *Cervantès Dramaturge: Un théâtre à naître* (Paris: Presses Universitaires de France, 1977), 58–59.

47. Miguel de Cervantes Saavedra, *La gran sultana Doña Catalina de Oviedo,* in *Teatro completo,* ed. Florencio Sevilla Arroyo and Antonio Rey Hazas (Barcelona: Planeta, 1987), l. 1217. Subsequent citations appear parenthetically in the text by line number only (line numbering is continuous in this edition).

48. Albert Mas, *Les Turcs dans la Littérature Espagnole du Siècle d'Or,* 2 vols. (Paris: Centre des Recherches Hispaniques, 1967), 1:342–344; and Canavaggio, *Cervantes Dramaturge,* 60–64.

49. In some ways, Catalina seems to be a less powerful figure than Bess, the heroine who exacts profitable trading terms for England from the Moroccan ruler Mullisheg in Thomas Heywood's contemporary play *The Fair Maid of the West.* While Catalina is shown helping individual Christians, she never improves conditions for Spaniards or even for Christians in general. For a reading of *Fair Maid* in relation to national identity, see Jean Howard, "An English Lass amid the Moors: Gender, Race, Sexuality, and National Identity in Heywood's *The Fair Maid of the West,*" in *Women, "Race," and Writing in the Early Modern Period,* ed. Hendricks and Parker, 102.

50. For religious freedom in North Africa, see Friedman, *Spanish Captives,* 89–90.

51. Mariscal, "*La gran sultana,*" 201.

52. Anderson, "Playing at Moslem and Christian," 53.

53. For the single-sex Galenic model, see Thomas Laqueur, *Making Sex* (Cambridge, Mass.: Harvard University Press, 1990). Stephen Greenblatt cites Montaigne and Paré in "Fiction and Friction," in *Shakespearean Negotiations: The Circulation of Social Energy in Renaissance England* (Berkeley: University of California Press, 1988), 66–93. A discussion of sexual transformations also appears in Antonio de Torquemada, *Jardín de flores curiosas* (1570; reprint, Madrid: Castalia, 1982), 187–91; and Juan Huarte de San Juan, *Examen de ingenios para las ciencias* (1575; reprint, Madrid: Nacional, 1976), 315–16. On hermaphroditism in early modern Spain as a kind of *mestizaje* that challenges "hegemonic Hispanism," see Israel Burshatin, "Interrogating Hermaphroditism in Sixteenth-Century Spain," in *Hispanisms and Homosexualities,* ed. Sylvia Molloy and Robert McKee Irwin (Durham, N.C.: Duke University Press, 1998), 3–18; and Burshatin, "Written on the Body."

Chapter 5: "La disimulación es provechosa"

1. In his preface to Heliodorus's *Aethiopica,* Cervantes's vaunted model for the *Persiles,* the French critic and translator Jacques Amyot praises "disguised histories"— fictions disguised as true history—for their verisimilitude. What I am interested in here is the central place of disguise and dissimulation within the narrative itself and, more broadly, Cervantes's fictional disguise of the historical preoccupation with "transparent" or easily legible identities. For a discussion of Amyot's preface, see Alban Forcione, *Cervantes, Aristotle, and the Persiles* (Princeton, N.J.: Princeton University Press, 1970), 55–64.

2. On the importance of "clean blood" for holding public office, see Kamen, *Inquisition and Society;* and Sicroff, *Los estatutos.* For Cervantes's own problematic relationship to this institutionalized discrimination, see Ellen Lokos, "The Politics of Identity and the Enigma of Cervantine Genealogy," in *Cervantes and His Postmodern Constituencies,* ed. Cruz and Johnson, 116–33.

3. For the notion of Antonio's offspring as mestizos, see George Mariscal, *"Persiles* and the Remaking of Spanish Culture," *Cervantes* 10 (1990): 93–102; and Mariscal, "The Crisis of Hispanism as Apocalyptic Myth," in *Cervantes and His Postmodern Constituencies,* ed. Cruz and Johnson, 201–17.

4. Alban Forcione, *Cervantes' Christian Romance* (Princeton, N.J.: Princeton University Press, 1972).

5. Antonio Márquez, "La ideología de Cervantes: El paradigma del *Persiles," Insula* 467 (n.d.): 1.

6. Taurisa, Auristela's servant, first tells us that Auristela claimed a vow of virginity to discourage Arnaldo (56). Arnaldo himself then refers to an unspecified vow to be fulfilled in Rome (124).

7. Forcione, *Cervantes' Christian Romance,* 108.

8. For a reading of these interpolated narratives as exemplary novels on love and marriage, see Diana de Armas Wilson, *Allegories of Love,* chaps. 7–10. Wilson's classification is based on thematic similarities. Her reading stresses the stories' broader exemplarity rather than any one allegorical narrative.

9. Márquez, "La ideología de Cervantes," 1.

10. On Cervantes's own use of this technique, see David Quint, "Narrative Interlace and Narrative Genres in *Don Quijote* and the *Orlando Furioso," Modern Language Quarterly* 58:3 (September 1997): 241–68. On the dynamic of error and dilation in romance, see Parker, *Inescapable Romance.*

11. See E. C. Riley, *Cervantes' Theory of the Novel* (Oxford: Clarendon, 1962), 120–21; Forcione, *Cervantes, Aristotle, and the Persiles,* 187–95; and Stanislav Zimic, "El *Persiles* como crítica de la novela bizantina," *Acta Neophilologica* 3 (1970): 49–64.

12. Zimic, "El *Persiles,"* 50, citing Américo Castro, *El pensamiento de Cervantes* (Madrid: Hernando, 1925), 95.

13. Mary Gaylord, "Ending and Meaning in Cervantes' *Persiles and Sigismunda," Romanic Review* 74.2 (1983): 152–69.

14. Sicroff, *Los estatutos,* 160.

15. The vagueness at the start of *Don Quijote*—"En un lugar de la Mancha de cuyo nombre no quiero acordarme" (31) (In a town of La Mancha, whose name I would not recall)—marks a certain coyness about origins that Américo Castro suggestively links to the *converso* experience. See Castro, "Cervantes y el *Quijote* a nueva luz," in *Cervantes y los casticismos españoles* (Madrid: Alianza, 1974), 61.

16. Lope de Rueda, *Comedia Medora,* quoted in Castro, "Cervantes y el *Quijote,"* 35.

17. Quevedo, *Libro de todas las cosas,* quoted in Castro, "Cervantes y el *Quijote,"* 35. Sicroff observes: "Cuando de pronto nos encontramos con una laguna inesperada en nuestros conocimientos sobre un personaje destacado, sobre todo en algo relativo a la

identidad de sus padres, o cuando vemos a ese personaje viajar sin cesar de una villa a otra, o mostrar un gusto curioso por vivir en el extranjero, debemos preguntarnos si tenemos delante a un cristiano nuevo que hace todo lo posible por borrar toda huella de su origen judío" (*Los estatutos*, 313) (When we suddenly find an unexpected gap in our knowledge of a well-known figure, especially where it concerns the identity of his parents, or when we see that figure travel ceaselessly from one town to the next or display a strange taste for living abroad, we must ask ourselves whether this is a case of a New Christian doing everything possible to erase all traces of his Jewish origins).

18. For critics of the *limpieza* investigations, see Sicroff, *Los estatutos*, chaps. 4–5.

19. The powerful discourse of inherited nobility in Counter-Reformation Spain in fact coexisted with a discourse of individual virtue, proposed by such thinkers as Fadrique Furió Ceriol, Fray Agustín Salucio, and Huarte de San Juan. See, for example, Mariscal, *Contradictory Subjects*, 31–53.

20. Elsewhere, Cervantes appears resolutely skeptical on the question of spells and witchcraft. In the novella "El licenciado Vidriera," for example, the narrator undercuts his explanation for Tomás's madness even as he narrates it: "una morisca, en un membrillo toledano dio a Tomás uno destos que llaman hechizos, creyendo que la daba cosa que le forzase la voluntad a quererla: como si hubiese en el mundo yerbas, encantos ni palabras suficientes a forzar el libre albedrío" (52) (a Morisca gave Tomás one of these they call spells in a Toledo quince, in the belief that what she gave him would force him to love her, as though there were in the world herbs, charms, or words that could force one's free will).

21. Cenotia's plea would have multiple resonances for a Spanish audience in 1617, shortly after the Morisco expulsions. For the connections between Petrarchan poetics and the discourse of empire in the period, see Roland Greene, *Unrequited Conquests: Love and Empire in the Colonial Americas* (Chicago: University of Chicago Press, 1999).

22. See, for example, the Morisco Jarife's speech (359), which I discuss below. In their 1492 edict expelling the Jews from Spain, Ferdinand and Isabella explicitly blame Jews for making Christians abandon Catholicism: "nos fuimos informados que en estos nuestros reynos abia algunos malos christianos que judaiçaban y apostataban de nuestra santa fee catolica, de lo qual hera mucha causa la comunicaçion de los judios con los christianos. . . . consta e parece el gran daño que a los christianos se a seguido e sigue de la participaçion, conbersaçion, comunicaçion que han tenido e tienen con los judios" (*Documentos acerca de la expulsión de los judíos*, ed. Luis Suárez Fernández [Valladolid: Consejo Superior de Investigaciones Científicas, 1964], 392) (we were informed that there were in our kingdoms bad Christians who practiced Judaism and apostatized from our holy Catholic faith, which was largely caused by the Jews' contact with the Christians. . . . the great damage to Christians from the participation, conversation, and communication that they have or have had with Jews is apparent).

The language of sinful contagion also appears frequently in the case of the Moriscos. The emphasis here is often on an almost animalistic fecundity, as in Jarife's speech. Fray Marcos de Guadalajara y Javier, in *Memorable expulsión y justísimo destierro de los moriscos de España* (1613), describes the Moriscos' "'pestilencia pegajosa'" (sticky pestilence) and urges the importance of not permitting that "'su contagión se pegue a los demás'" (their contagion stick to others). Pedro Aznar Cardona, in *Expulsión justificada de los moriscos españoles* (1612), describes them thus: "'Estos eran los lobos en las ovejas, los zánganos en la colmena, los cuervos entre palomas, los perros en la Iglesia, los gitanos entre los israelitas y finalmente los herejes entre los católicos'" (These were the wolves in the fold, the drones in the hive, the ravens among doves, the dogs in the Church, the gypsies among the Israelites, and, finally, the heretics among the Catholics). Both are quoted in Louis Cardaillac, "Vision simplificatrice des groupes marginaux," in *Les problèmes de l'exclusion*, ed. Redondo, 12.

23. Wilson, *Allegories of Love*, 3. For Cervantes's relation to Heliodorus, see Rudolph Schevill, "*Persiles y Sigismunda*: The Question of Heliodorus," *Modern Philology* 4 (1906–7): 677–704; Wilson, *Allegories of Love*, 3–23; and Forcione, *Cervantes, Aristotle, and the Persiles*.

24. On the sixteenth-century canonization of Heliodorus, see Forcione, *Cervantes, Aristotle, and the Persiles*, 49–85; and Wilson, *Allegories of Love*, 20–23.

25. Constance Hubbard Rose, *Alonso Núñez de Reinoso: The Lament of a Sixteenth-Century Exile* (Rutherford, N.J.: Fairleigh Dickinson University Press, 1971), 10.

26. See Stanislav Zimic, "Leucipe y Clitofonte y Clareo y Florisea en el *Persiles* de Cervantes," *Anales cervantinos* 13–14 (1974–75): 37–58; and Javier Gonzalez Rovira, *La novela bizantina española* (Madrid: Gredos, 1996).

27. Alonso Núñez de Reinoso, *Historia de los amores de Clareo y Florisea y de los trabajos de la sin ventura Isea*, ed. Carlos Aribau (Madrid: Rivadeneyra, 1876), 446. Subsequent references to this edition appear parenthetically in the text, by page number.

28. Garcilaso de la Vega, "Egloga III," in *Poesías castellanas completas*, ed. Elías L. Rivers (Madrid: Castalia, 1996), ll. 246–48.

29. See especially Rose, *Alonso Núñez de Reinoso*, chaps. 3–4.

30. Ibid., 125–28. Covarrubias first gives the religious meaning, "El que sale de su tierra en romería a visitar alguna casa santa o lugar santo," and then expands upon it, "Peregrinar, andar en romería o fuera de su tierra" (*Tesoro de la lengua*, 863).

31. On the representation of Auristela and her portraits, see Gaylord, "Ending and Meaning." Periandro's canvas recalls also the episode of the false captives, students who imitate the heroism of Christian captives in North Africa simply to make money (bk. 3, chap. 10). See my discussion of this episode in *Mimesis and Empire*, chap. 6.

32. René Quérillacq analyzes Jarife's speech in conjunction with Ricote's to mark the irony in both ("Los moriscos de Cervantes," *Anales cervantinos* 30 [1992]: 77–98).

33. Mariscal, "*Persiles* and the Remaking of Spanish Culture," 97. See also Mariscal, "Crisis of Hispanism."

34. Mariscal, "*Persiles* and the Remaking of Spanish Culture," 100.

35. Rafael Lapesa, "'La española inglesa' y el *Persiles*," in *De la edad media a nuestros días* (Madrid: Gredos, 1967), 258.

36. Carroll B. Johnson, "'La española inglesa' and the Practice of Literary Production," *Viator* 19 (1988): 377–416.

37. Castro, *El pensamiento de Cervantes*, 302.

38. On Isabela as a *conversa,* see Manuel da Costa Fontes, "Love as an Equalizer in 'La española inglesa,'" *Romance Notes* 16.1 (Autumn 1974): 742–48.

39. Ibid., 744.

40. Johnson points out the theological irony of a Protestant queen requiring that a Catholic subject prove himself through works ("'La española inglesa,'" 399).

41. On the interchangeability of national styles and Ricaredo's merging of categories, see ibid., 396–98.

42. On *reducción* as "the submission of the schismatic and heretic to the authority of Rome," see Thomas Hanrahan, "History in the *Española inglesa,*" *Modern Language Notes* 83 (1968): 267–71.

Index

Index

Index

BARBARA FUCHS is an associate professor of Romance languages at the University of Pennsylvania. She is the author of *Mimesis and Empire: The New World, Islam, and European Identities* (2001) as well as articles in *Cervantes, Shakespeare Quarterly, English Literary History,* and other journals.

~ *Hispanisms*

Cervantes and the Material World   *Carroll B. Johnson*
Spain in America: The Origins of Hispanism in the United States   *Edited by*
   Richard L. Kagan
Passing for Spain: Cervantes and the Fictions of Identity   *Barbara Fuchs*

The University of Illinois Press
is a founding member of the
Association of American University Presses.

─────────────────────────────

Composed in 10.5/13 Minion
with Minion display
by Jim Proefrock
at the University of Illinois Press
Designed by Dennis Roberts
Manufactured by Thomson-Shore, Inc.

University of Illinois Press
1325 South Oak Street
Champaign, IL 61820-6903
www.press.uillinois.edu